The Art of
Papermaking
with Plants

Please note that bleach and caustic soda are hazardous
materials. It is the reader's responsibility to always wear
gloves and proper eye protection when working with
these materials.

Certain recipes call for plants or trees not indigenous to
the United States. If you use another plant in its place,
you may have to adapt the recipe accordingly.

Translated by Andrea Costella

Copyright © 2002 by Éditions du Rouergue
English translation copyright © 2004 by
W. W. Norton & Company, Inc.

Originally published in French as *L'Art du Papier Végétal*

For information about permission to reproduce selections from
this book, write to Permissions, W. W. Norton & Company, Inc.,
500 Fifth Avenue, New York, NY 10110

Composition by Ken Gross
Manufacturing by Eurografica

Library of Congress Cataloging-in-Publication Data

Lorenté, Marie-Jeanne.
    [Art du papier végétal. English]
    The art of papermaking with plants / Marie-Jeanne Lorenté; photographs
by Vincent Decorde; illustrations by Sophie Beltran and Hippolyte Coste.
       p.   cm.
    Translation of: L'art du papier végétal.
    Includes bibliographical references.
    ISBN: 0-393-73135-9 (pbk.)
    1. Papermaking. I. Title.

TS1105.L6713   2004
676'.22–dc21   2003052747

W. W. Norton & Company, Inc., 500 Fifth Avenue, New York, N.Y. 10110
www.wwnorton.com

W. W. Norton & Company Ltd., Castle House, 75/76 Wells St., London W1T 3QT

0 9 8 7 6 5 4 3 2 1

The Art of Papermaking with Plants

Marie-Jeanne Lorenté

Photographs by Vincent Decorde

Illustrations by Sophie Beltran and Hippolyte Coste

W. W. Norton & Company
New York • London

A book of spells for plant magicians.

Marie-Jeanne Lorenté

For Chloé and Boris

Contents

Trees

Edible Plants

Non-plant Papers

Nine artists of plant paper

Conversion of Measurements

US Unit	UK Imperial Unit	Metric
1 pint	0.832 pint	473.2 milliliters
1 liter	1.76 pints	1,000 milliliters
1 quart	1.665 pints	946.3 milliliters
1 fluid ounce	1.041 fluid ounces	29.57 milliliters

The Essence of
Plant Paper

The pleasures of paper

It is the nearly nothing
the fragility
or rather, the fragilities.

It creases, rips, burns, dampens . . .
and disappears, decomposes.

If song is the music of the soul,
paper is its mold, its caress, its memory,
its thought . . .
materialized, realized.

Supple, and at once solid and fragile, it has
the same qualities as humans.
It is our mirror.

Elm leaf

Plant paper

only exists among artists, miracle-workers, fairies and their twin sisters . . . magicians.

In reality, all paper is plant-based because it is produced from wood at industrial plants, from cotton cloths, flax, or from the hemp of artisans. But the creators of vegetable paper work neither in factories nor in papermaking mills. Their "miracles" occur in kitchens, in the corners of garages, or in workrooms.

They are neither scientists, botanists, chemists, nor ecologists, though they have a true regard for nature.

They are merely inventors, transformers, and magicians.

These handmade papers are of human creation—no need for a chainsaw, a shredder, or other machine.

Patience and passion suffice, though a bit of curiosity helps.

This is paper made from skin and peelings, and therein lies the miracle.

Make handsome sheets of paper, large or small, with plants found along roadsides, bordering water, or from the leaves of trees, in a pot or a basin, with your hands.

We wander the fields in the early morning hours.

We disappear under an armful of perfumed plants.

We feel our way around.

We cut, peel, and cook for hours and hours.

Intoxicated by a million scents, but happy.

We create anything that strikes our fancy, without limits or censure.

We invent our own aesthetic vocabulary.

Let these notes, these recipes, be only the starting point—incitements.

Creating paper gives us the power to be closer to ourselves. Without regard to duration, eternity, or what is conventional and acceptable.
Let's be neither classical nor modern.
Let's not be artists, but let's not fear being artists.
Let's be ourselves.
Let's imagine a medium for our creations and achieve it without self-censorship.

There is no hierarchy in papermaking: the most successful sheets of paper are neither the most beautiful, nor the most ugly, but the best adapted to our idea.

We are free to make whatever it is we want to say.

Invent paper from scarlet pimpernel, cyprus spurge, arum, asphodel, water lilies, grape hyacinth, and lily of the valley.

Create lily of the valley paper for pleasure, for the poetic idea, for everything and for nothing.

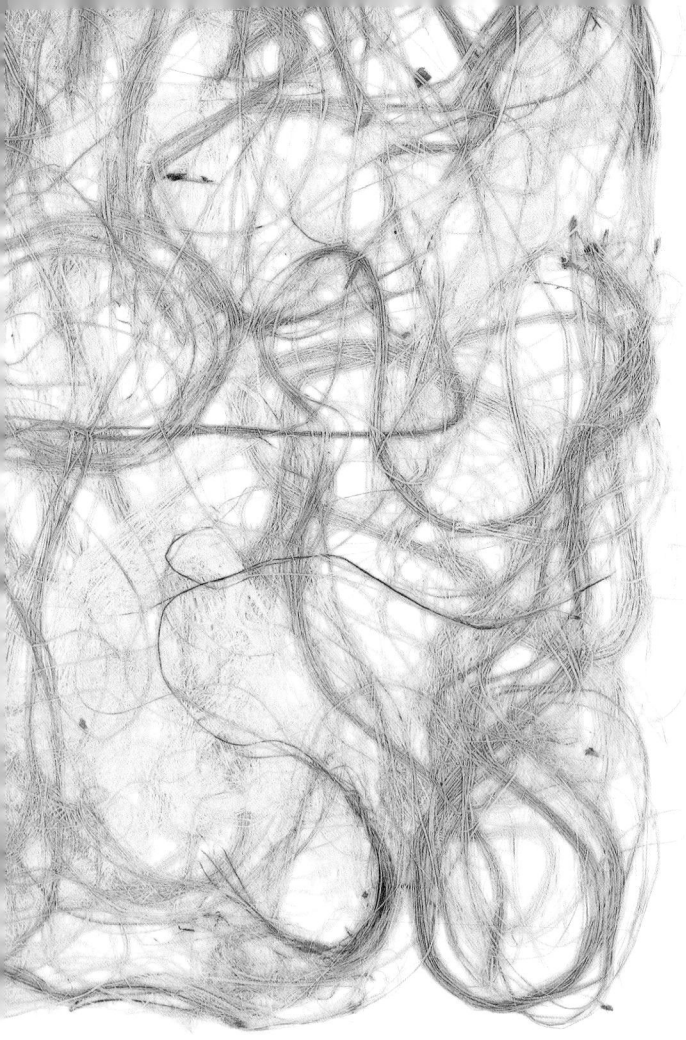

Replace utilitarian paper with paper that pleases.

Did you know that paper made from spiderwort is extremely rare? In fact, spiderwort, a plant full of water, melts like butter in the sun, and each time you cook it only a few fibers, both precious and rather shabby, remain.

And so life goes, with all its injustices.

But wheat paper? Wheat paper is a wonder of profitability: One pot of raw wheat when cooked equals one pot of paper pulp—or nearly.

Everything in the wheat stalk is useful—use the wheat grains to make cardboard, or leave them out to make paper.

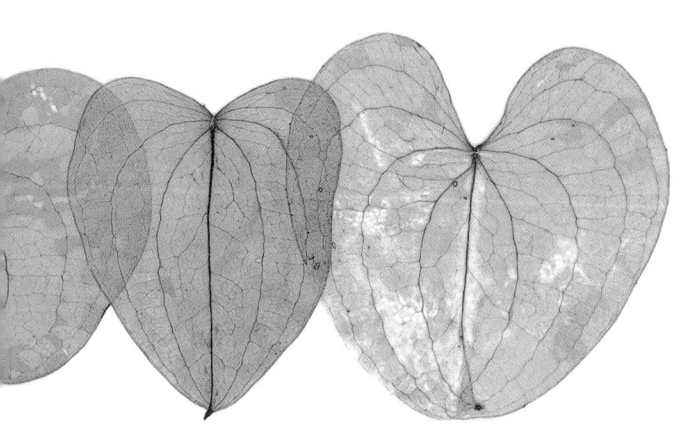

Sarsaparilla

Presentation

A green sheet
of paper.
I move close to it:
Bits of yellow and blue.
A murmur,
The wild oat leaf tells its story.

The meadowsweet reveals several traits
after it is cooked for the first time.
Yellow—part gentleness, part rage.
Gleaming and subtle at the same time.
The paradoxical meadowsweet.

Then the indigo plant, sovereign blue, and yet
somewhat green.
Indigo camouflages itself, hides its spirit.
Indigo is green, intense.
But even the lightest things flirt with the air, and the
air transforms them, giving them life.
Indigo sees life in blue as soon as it spreads itself out
and breathes,
with a tinge of red, for passion.
This nearly violet, with some yellow, turns to green,
once again.

I like the stories of the wild oat leaf.
Sometimes while needlepointing,
I like to be its confidante.
I dare to talk to it and tell it my story.
With silk, to make it pardon the violent
penetration of my needle.
An eternal, silky mildness follows.
Day-to-day life with plants reminds me
that I am not an afterthought,
I am an integral part of Nature.
I can converse with her.

Plant paper knows how to tell its stories to those
who know how to listen.

The Magical Essence

The ritual begins with the gathering of the plants and ends in the enjoyment of creation.

In the meantime, we can delight in various transformations:

• Humans in our desire for poetic achievements.
• Paper magicians for being able to transform gurgling, smelly, cooking plants.
• Fairies for changing leaves (of trees) into leaves (of paper).
• Humans in the satisfaction of having created something personal.

Expression, therefore, can exist at last on and in the paper.

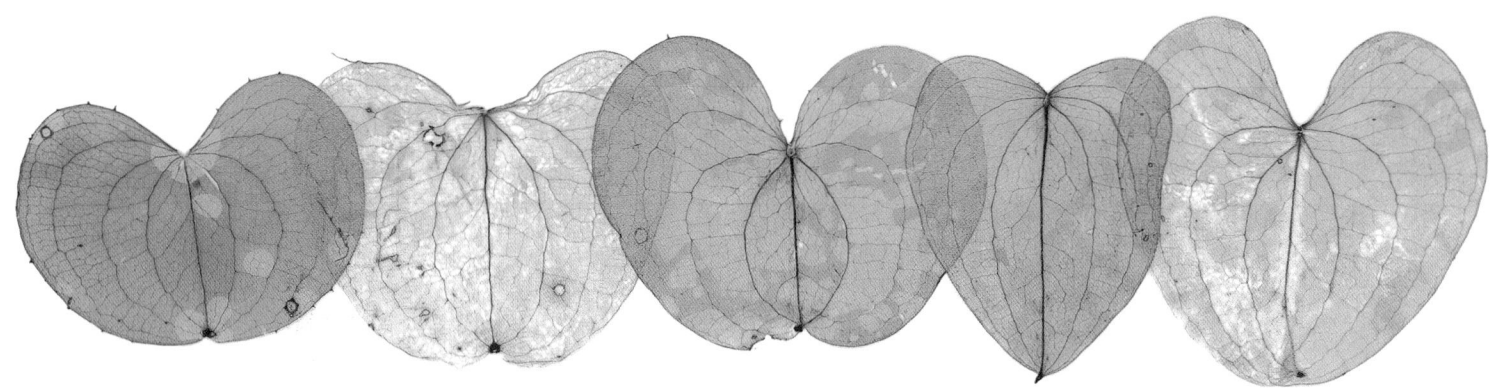

The Practical Essence

The more practical craftsperson will achieve:
• greeting and anniversary cards, party invitations . . .
• paper on which to write, dream, calculate, tell stories . . .
• lamps for seeing and illuminating . . .
• bookmarks to keep, touch, insert . . .
• books, notepads, notebooks containing a collection of dried flowers . . .
• jewelry, hats, bags, ready-to-wear clothes . . .

The Poetic Essence

Stinging nettle, one of the worst kinds of weeds, enchants as it transforms itself into a soft, immaculately white silk.

The extravagance of wild oat leaves remains forever engraved in a nearly white, pulpy base.

Wild fennel and lavender lose their fragrance but mark paper indelibly with their ragged stems.

The iris develops its plant fibers subtly and elegantly, delightfully encircling our fingers. In the end, its leaves are sprawling, its fringes long or short, but even the most recalcitrant are profoundly moving. The plant fibers are not completely smooth—their relief accentuated by brilliant mysteriousness—and they celebrate, victorious claimers of obvious happiness.

Pampas grass transforms itself into lace on which our love notes can be written, while paper from garlic or the thorny cactus signals an end to our romances. The chestnut tree and the elm do not hesitate to undress, showing us, without shame, their anatomy—a gossamer skeleton—that is only relatively fragile;

they crease and straighten out like an old, adored shirt.

The hornbeam tree is a small miracle unto itself; its appearance is very distinct (with straight dark veins); it feels lighter, finer than silk, it weighs nothing, it contents itself with stroking the scales, stealing from and challenging gravity.

grass paper
canna paper
woodrush paper
field horsetail paper
lentisk (mastic tree) paper
boxwood paper
rose petal paper

And tomorrow . . .

Paper made from ferns, reeds, yucca leaves, autumn crocuses, papyrus, pumpkins, artichokes, leeks, Swiss chard, onions, asparagus, wild myrtle, wild oat leaves, silver birches, maples, pine trees, poplars, lime trees, palm trees, bay leaves, olive trees, ginkgo leaves . . .

The Invention of Paper

In A.D. 105 in China, Tsaï Lun, a high functionary in the Han court, codified the production of paper and became its official inventor. However, even older paper dates from 206 B.C., made from hemp, the bark of blackberry bushes, bamboo, rice straw, and sandalwood. The mystery of paper's origin continues.

Legend has it that Tsaï Lun invented paper after observing a wasp construct its nest from paper.

The secret to making paper remained in that part of the world for centuries.

In 794, when the Japanese had 180 varieties, the Western world still had not been introduced to paper.

The association between paper and writing was made immediately, signifying an immense progress.

No more bamboo—crumbly
silk—expensive
stone—heavy
papyrus—fragile

Holly

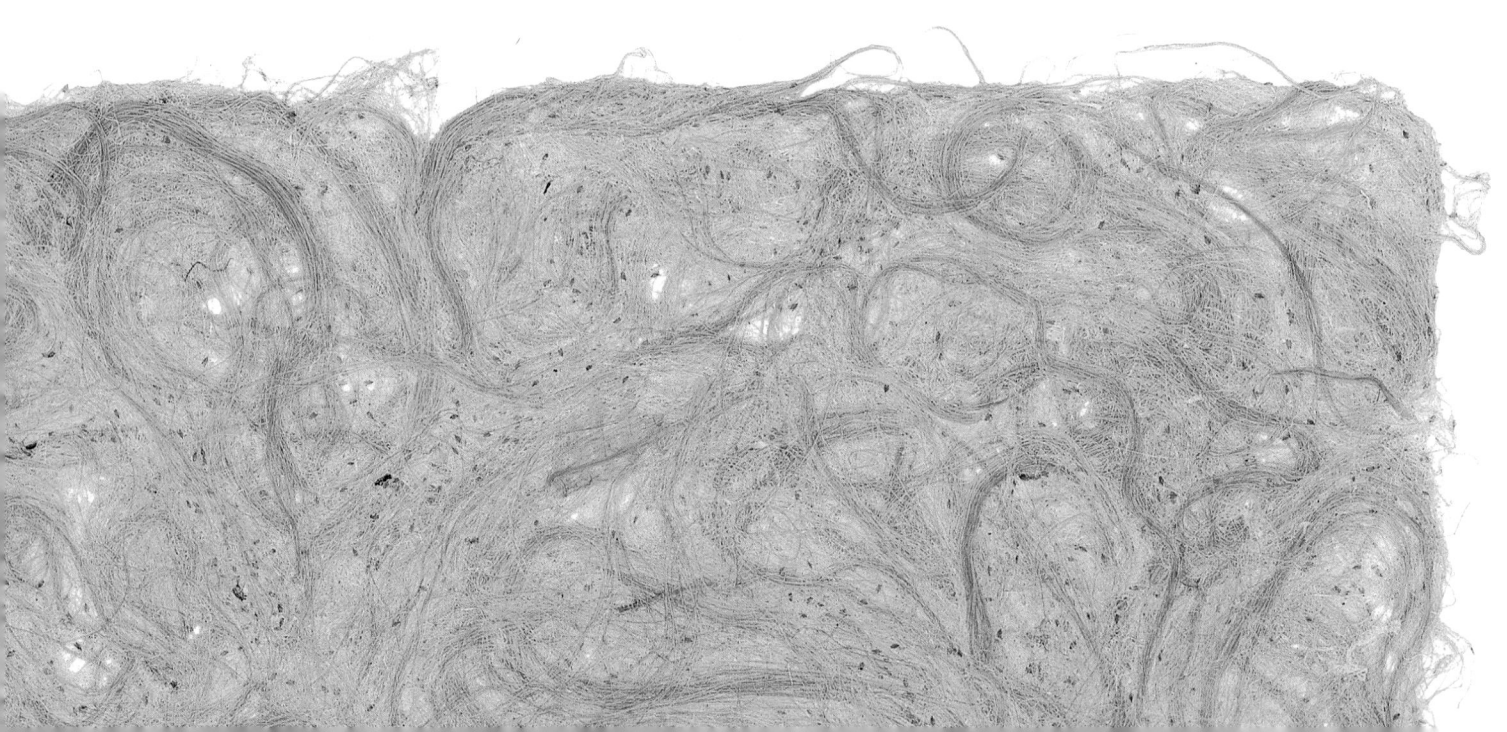

Parchment, which so inspired our imaginations, was also cast aside.

But we acquired: paper hens, postcards, gift cards, playing cards, puppets, music for mechanical pianos, wrapping paper, candy wrappers, confetti . . .

There is no need for words in order to recognize the dreamer behind paper hens, the generosity behind the gift, the gourmand behind the candy, the reveler behind confetti and other decorations. The artist is unique in his or her work.

In 751, Turkistan—until then China—came under the control of a caliph from Baghdad. The Chinese prisoners passed on their knowledge of paper. The Arabs improved it and invented paper made from cloth, which we still produce today. Between 794 and 795, the first paper factory was established in Baghdad under Hanoun-al Rashid, the caliph of "a thousand and one nights." When the Arabs imprisoned the Chinese papermakers, they didn't doubt that these war "treasures" had something more to offer. They very quickly grasped the economic, social, and cultural contributions of paper. The Arabs commercialized it throughout the Mediterranean basin, then established paper mills in Andalusia (since the seventh century, Spain had been under Moorish influence), in Sicily, Italy, and France—in all commercially strategic regions and in areas rich in necessary resources (forests, rivers).

Today, when I ask a manufacturer the dimensions of the largest sheet of paper, he responds that the numbers are inaccurate. If a size could be determined—presumably the size of the machine producing it—the machine could continue its production indefinitely, implying a sheet of paper of infinite length. Infinite.

Infinite does not seem part of something concrete or material.

For me, only love is infinite, so I like the idea that paper flirts with the infinity of time and space.

The phenomenon of paper really takes off at the end of the nineteenth century: In the United States walls are produced in paper, caskets, roads, horseshoes—all in paper. And let us not forget the paper church from Downsham-in-the-Isle in England, circa 1895.

But it was the Japanese who set the tone by producing paper so early: paper armor, paper blankets, glossy paper outfits, coats of oiled paper, hats and shoes from paper pulp. For them, the papermaker, working with material so elevated and noble, must be sincere, honest, and pure in his work.

What was Issey Miyake doing when he presented collections of dresses in paper, if not subscribing to the traditions of his native country? Undergarments made from paper. Like a second skin.

All of this shows us to what extent paper makes us imagine.

The destiny of paper, however, was incontestably the book. Gutenberg is the official "father" of printing. Yet, the first printed book made with movable, metal type appeared in 1390 in China—nearly a century before Gutenberg's discovery.

One would be tempted to say that from this moment on, the printing press hurried progress: the speed of rag-paper production becomes frenetic. Paper mills are built everywhere.

Interest in books rapidly evolves. The reader demands accessible, swift information. The French Revolution results in the freedom of press, a liberty which is inscribed in the Declaration of the Rights of Man of August, 1789.

Paper becomes the memory of the word.

After 1865, wood replaces rag for certain kinds of paper (for printing, notably writing).

Then industrial paper knocks at the door of progress, creating even greater demand.

In 1998, the world produced 175.5 million tons of paper pulp. Pulp is essentially produced from:
—the by-products of sawmills (30 percent) (wood chips and packing paper);
—the tops of trees or logs (34 percent); and
—logs from the first thinning (36 percent) for paper whose fibers are virgin.

More and more products are produced from recycled paper pulp: cartons, paper packages, magazines, journals—all retrieved, treated, and recycled. Today, this pulp represents 41.6 percent of paper production.

The oldest recycled paper was found in Japan, dating from 1031.

What became of our rag paper? Twenty years ago it represented 3 percent of French paper production. Today, it represents no more than 1 percent, reserved only for luxurious paper. We know that the future of paper is industrial. More and more furniture is being produced from paper, paper fertilizer, paper logs . . .

Even if information technology, which promises to put an end to paper in the twenty-first century, takes over the classical form of archives, it will not replace toilet paper, tissues, mailbox circulars, carnival masks, photos, paper towels, food wrapping, checks, or love letters that we keep close to our hearts for an eternity.

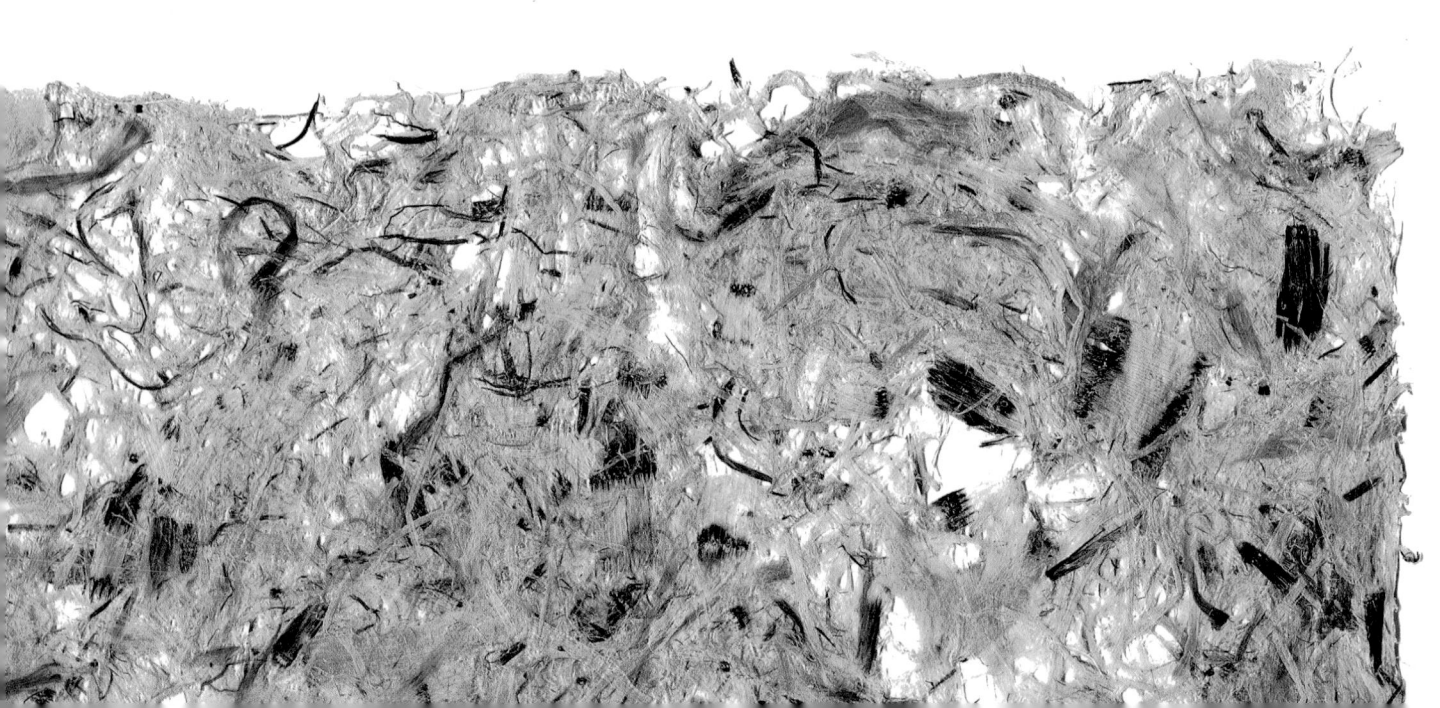

However, while the paper industry is constantly innovating—it even invented non-polluting production procedures—it is hard pressed to find managers responsible for installing these new procedures and machines, so that tomorrow we might be able to fish in the waters around the factories. We already know that healthy forest management allows paper mills to be constantly supplied with wood without harm to natural resources, and actually even regulates the greenhouse effect. The production of paper requires a large quantity of water. Water recycling and water purification systems can be installed in production units. Factories are treating and reusing water more and more. Pollution and deforestation are not inevitable; humans and political goodwill can keep our planet beautiful and clean.

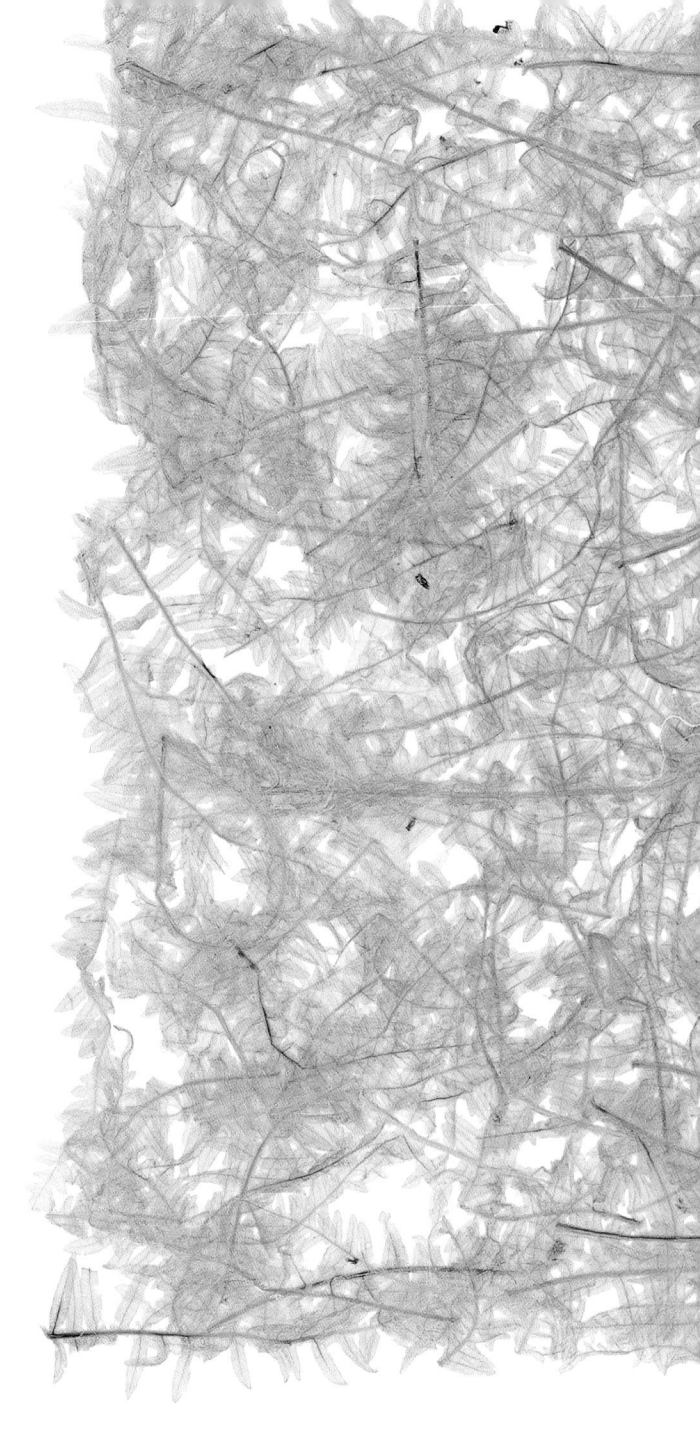

Chestnut leaves

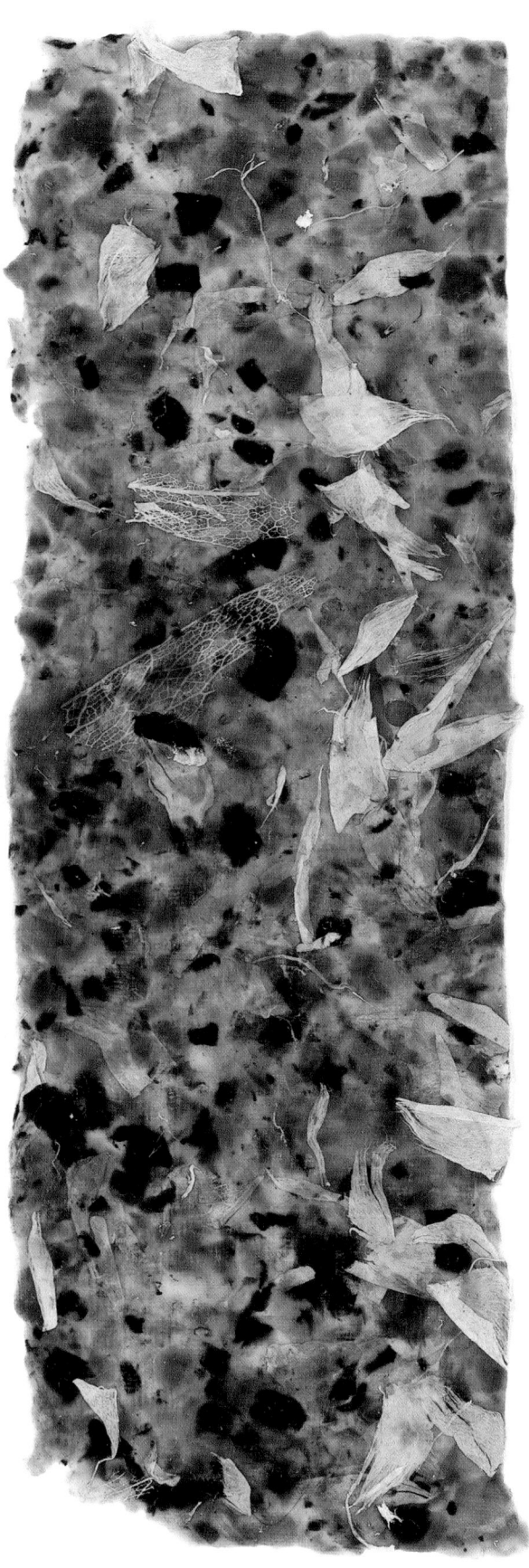

Transmitting the ephemeral

by Ernest Pignon Ernest

All the images that I create—original or silkscreen designs—are achieved on a very thin, particularly fragile paper: from rotary press newsprint. It's the only paper that, when soaked with glue, also manages to become malleable. I can make it hug the most complicated moldings, penetrate the smallest crack, introduce it into the tiniest crevice. When it dries, it reveals the texture of the wall to which it adheres, like a very fine skin. In a way, the paper integrates its medium with the image that it displays, or rather, it's the wall itself that absorbs the image and the image is left to return to its own medium. A man I once spoke with found the right words to describe the phenomenon. He explained to me, "One would say that your images seep into the wall."

Maybe he was thinking of Saint Suaire, of an apparition. These aren't exactly my sentiments, but it is true that this paper has something materially miraculous about it. In this sense, for me, paper is much more than layout space: its very substance achieves the physical bond, the material solidarity that I seek to construct between the image that I create and the wall on which it becomes visible.

The effect would be very different with poster board of 80 or 90 lbs (150 or 200 gsm), which would remain, in its flat and rigid inertia, on the surface of the medium. Even perfectly glued, poster board would, at best, "rest" on the wall, meaning that it would only assume the pose, turning its back to the wall to attach itself there as on an improvised picture rail . . . the exact opposite of what I search for. Conversely, newsprint, with its suppleness and the quality of the glue that is soaked up by it, becomes the epidermis of the wall, its interface, a pure boundary between the inside and the outside of the wall. It's really as much about the glue as about the paper: oil-based glues

that we use today, thick like varnish, no longer
have the quality of Rémy glue, liquid and
smooth, that cover and cross the paper,
allowing it to rediscover the primitive fluidity
of the paper pulp, unctuous and malleable. But
the paper only adheres to its medium to the
extent that its delicacy and quasi-immateriality
allow it; its extreme precariousness is always
there acting as a counterbalance.

I have toyed with this apparent fragility,
this vulnerability of paper, since my very first
projects, but it was only while studying
Rimbaud that I integrated these projects into
my research as an essential element of my
artistic plan. Since adolescence, I have been
struck by a sort of disconcerting notion. The
idea of rendering an artistic, living image of
Rimbaud consumes me, but I feel, in a way,
that this would serve to deny Rimbaud more
than to fix him in a painting of his own
identity. Imagine a Rimbaud in marble, or
dripping in bronze! Paper, silk screen—the
multiplicity of images (so true it is that the
same design doesn't say the same thing,
installed on Place Charleville or along a
highway)—and, even more so, their fore-
seeable and irreparable destruction, allowed
me to create a portrait at once repeatable (I've
glued hundreds), incomplete, erratic, and
resolutely perishable. A work, by definition, is
never finished, having no totality in space or
time, and even more so, a work is destined to
disappear. It is this very idea that paper, with
its multiple dimensions and in its fundamental
fragility, permits us to affirm. The power of
paper is like the paradoxical power of a
painting—unrecoverable and not localizable—
that wishes for its own disappearance.
Essentially, if there were some Rimbaldian
element to it all, it is this sense of abandon to
which I would like to give feeling—like a
reference to an abandoned work—in which the
work cares only that it disappear purely and
simply from our horizon. The suspension of a
language.

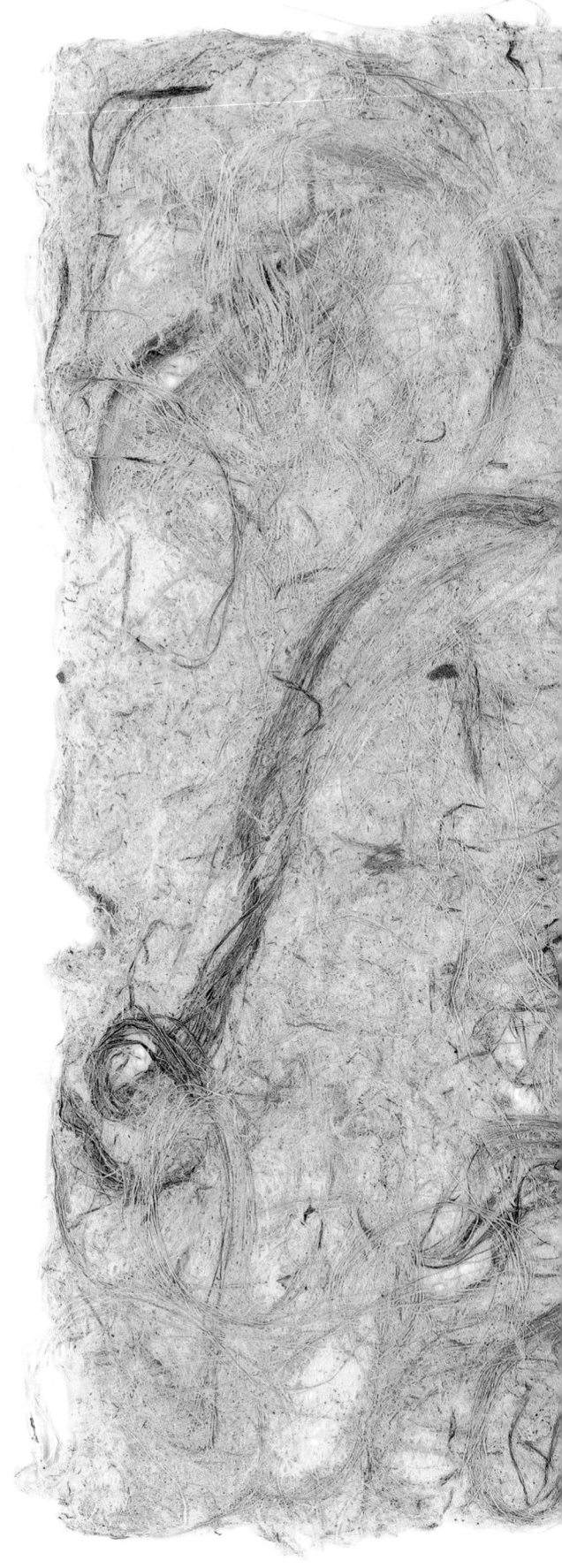

If these designs of mine are moving, it's really, I believe, because they are perceived with the certitude of their imminent and irreparable destruction: the evidence of their extreme precariousness is integral to the manner in which they are received and recognized. But this precariousness also constitutes, for me, an ethical demand from my work: the interaction between the design itself and its breakdown is only stronger because the design is charged with a rich and visual meaning. In this scenario, the conception and achievement of the work become even more intense because it is inherently doomed to an inevitable destruction.

I have worked particularly on this tension of ideas in Naples, with images associated with Easter, on the theme of death and its rapport with the buried. For example, I have installed on a road the image of a man carrying on his back a sagging body whose open hand dangles along the ground: the hand, collapsing to the bottom of the wall on which the image is affixed, fragile, bruised, dragging on the ground, is imprinted on a large sheet of this ephemeral and perishable paper whose underside is stuck straight to the ground. The tension I'm speaking about is not only relative to the strength of the design itself: it depends as much on the artistic and symbolic quality of the medium on which the image is placed. This type of image I placed only on roads paved with blacktop.

What I'm looking for is the confrontation between, on one hand, the extreme vulnerability of the image and the paper and, on the other hand, the visual and imaginary power that almost literally breaks forth from this black pavement extracted from volcano. Here again, for me, the impact of this artistic undertaking resides less in the design itself than in the decisive encounter between the image and where it appears: the dialogue between the underside and the surface, between the paper consecrated to immediate destruction and the organic density of the ground, black as the night, where the pains of history are inscribed in a rock vitrified by fire.

Ernest Pignon Ernest, *Desnos, Nerval*, drawings on blacktop, situated on rue Adolphe-Adam (where the poet Nerval committed suicide), Paris, 2001. Author's photo.

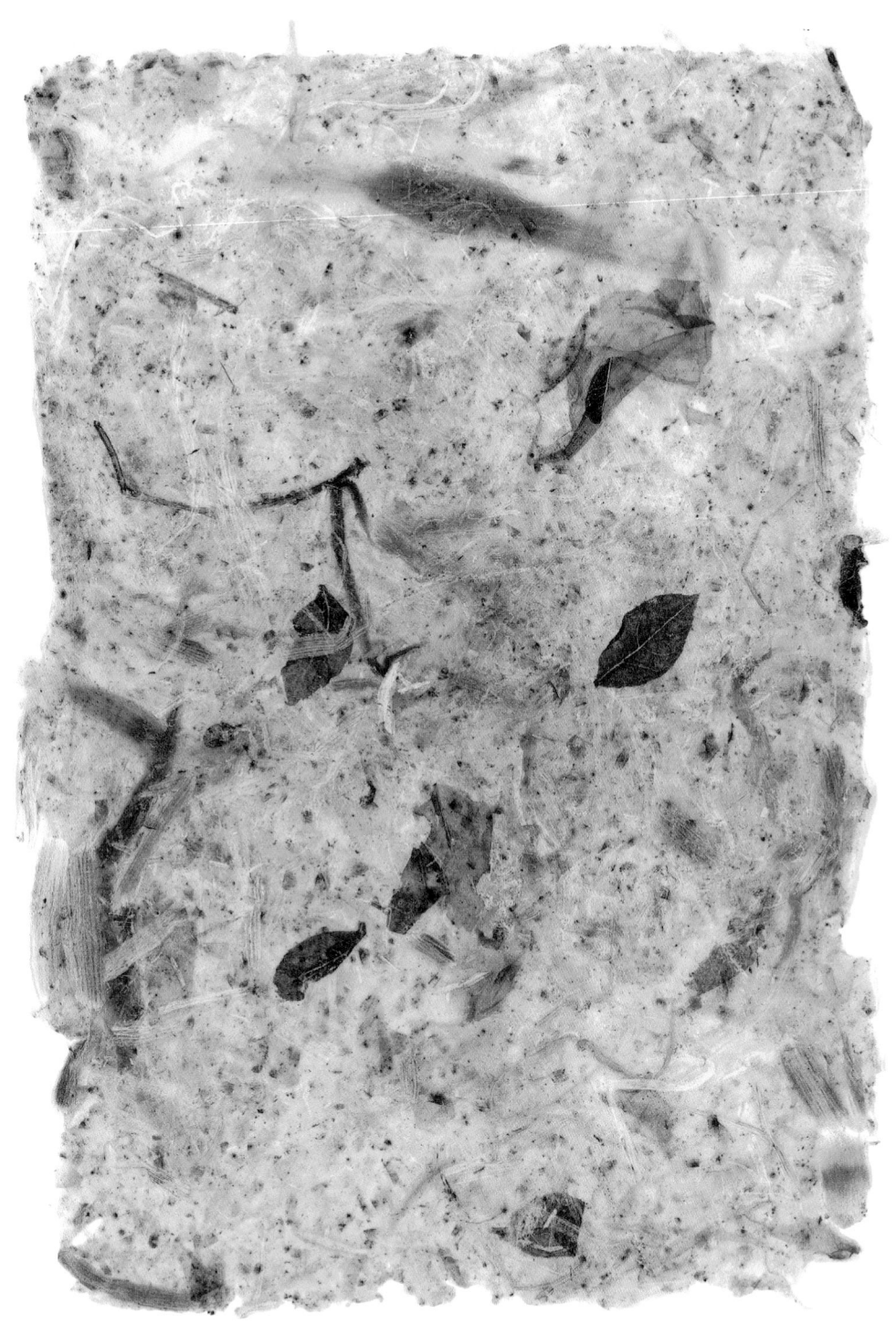

Production

Materials

- All-purpose scissors or a pair of secateurs

- Heavy-duty rubber gloves

- Matches or a lighter

- Stick for stirring

- Cylinder of gas

- Gas stove

- Pot

- Bottle

- Two colanders

- Basins of different size

- Two rags

- Sponge

- Bleach

- Screen (mold and deckle)

- Cardboard

- Press or clamp

- Plywood boards

- Caustic soda

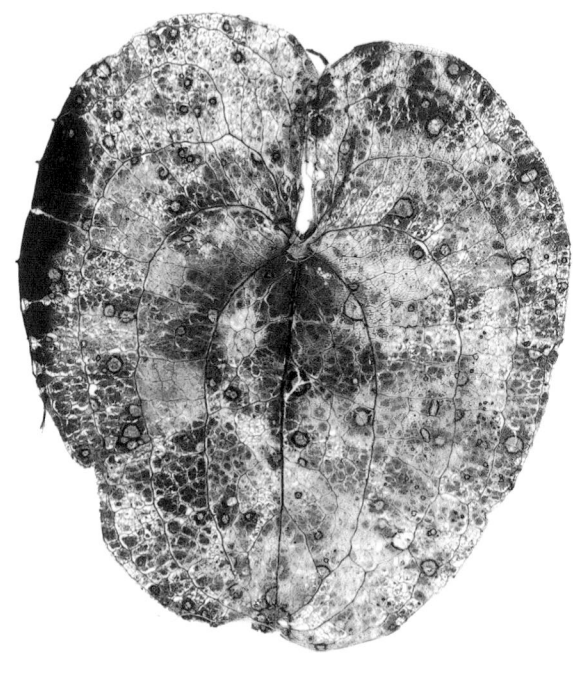

Scissors and secateurs

The quality of scissors or secateurs is very important to avoid ripping out the plants or damaging the branches.

Colanders

Use these to rinse the paper pulp. When working with tree leaves, kitchen strainers are ideal.

Basins

You'll need several:
• small, to contain the pulp,
• medium, to facilitate rinsing, and
• one larger than your mold and deckle in order to make the sheets of paper.

Gas burner and cylinder of gas

A portable gas burner and cylinder of gas are very practical because they allow you to perform the work wherever you like. A well-ventilated area is preferable to a small kitchen. Furthermore, a portable burner permits you to work close to the ground and therefore avoid accidents. When pots are full they are heavy and difficult to carry. Heavy-duty gloves are crucial for work with caustic soda and hot water. Regular rubber gloves are too fragile.

Pot

Choose a copper, stainless steel, or enameled iron pot. Avoid aluminum, which reacts with caustic soda.

Stick

A long stick is preferable to a wooden kitchen spoon so you don't splash yourself when you stir the plants.

Rags and press

Use fine, absorbent rags—old sheets, for example—cut to the same dimension as the press in order to work comfortably. Old engraving presses are very practical, and can still be found at second-hand dealers. If you don't have one, don't worry. You can create your own with two sheets of plywood and a clamp. This kind of press works best if you want to produce large sheets of paper.

Colander

Make your own colander or strainer with a laundry basket and mosquito netting. Sew together all the folds of the netting in the four corners of the colander. This is tedious work but necessary to prevent the paper pulp from seeping into the folds.

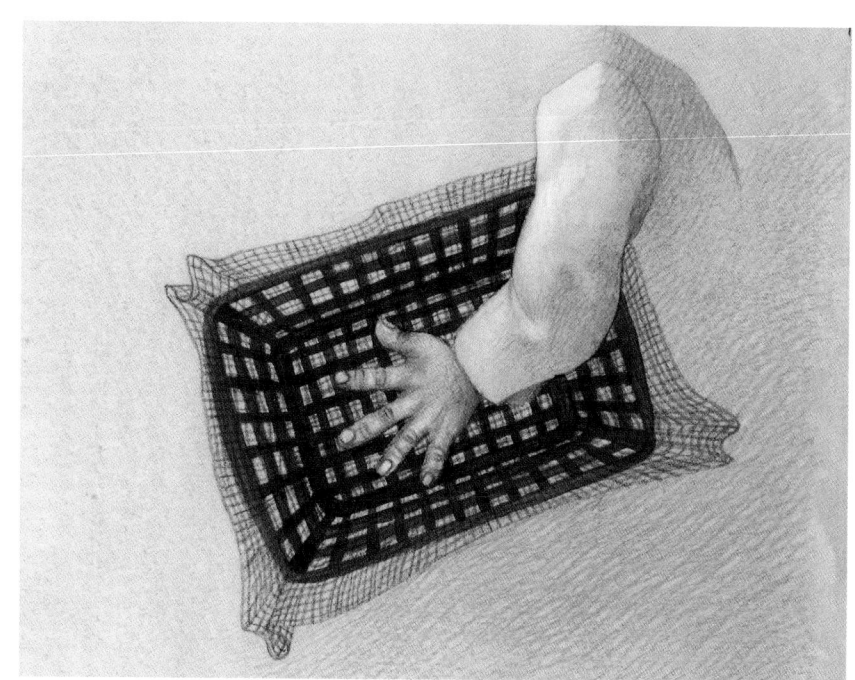

Screen
(mold and deckle)

Make your mold and deckle with wooden strips, mosquito netting (or another fine mesh, like woven fabric or finely woven phosphor bronze wire), and staples. Build two identical frames by securely gluing and stapling the corners together. Cover one of the two frames with the netting—this frame is the mold. Pull the netting tight and staple it to the wood. You can create your own unique mold shape: round, oval, hexagonal. The deckle is the second, uncovered frame that fits over the mold and determines the shape and thickness of the sheet of paper by preventing it from spilling over the sides of the mold. The mold and deckle won't cost you much, but the price of the material does not predict the end result.

You can create a personal watermark with brass wire filigree. Create a shape or design and sew it to the screen. It lends credibility, refines, and enlivens the paper.

Although the paper will be more fragile around the watermark, the watermark is the papermaker's signature—an act of reclaiming your work—whether you are an industrialist or artisan.

Certain watermarks are very simple, others are very sophisticated. Generally, they are images representative of their creators.

Procedure

If you live in the city, you can obtain the necessary plants and greenery from horticulturalists, florists, or with the help of parks department services.

Harvest

Plants

Pay attention to the seasons and the needs of the plants. For example:

- Bulbs need leaves in order to regenerate; do not cut their leaves before they have fallen to the ground.
- Do not harvest the plants too early in the season; the fibers will not be strong enough.

Note also that wild plants should not be removed without the proper authority. The conservation of wild plants is essential if they are to survive.

Leaves

Never cut the branches off trees. Harvest only the leaves, even if that requires you to reach up in the air for several minutes.

Wait until the end of spring or the beginning of summer to begin the papermaking process with leaves of deciduous trees; the fibers must be sufficiently firm to support the various treatments involved. For spectacular paper, gather leaves in the fall, just before peak foliage.

Preparation of the plants

Don't cut the plant into pieces that are too small; its unique shape and texture will not be as apparent. The fibers must be sufficiently long to ripple, yet short enough to avoid entanglement. Always cut stems shorter than the diameter of the pot in which you stir them—and stir gently to avoid overturning the pot.

The proportion of water to caustic soda

Caustic soda is available either dry and needing to be diluted, or in liquid form, in which case you may pour it directly in the basin of water as indicated in the recipes. The quantity of caustic soda you need depends on the quantity of water, which depends on the quantity of plants used. As a general rule, place the plants in an empty pot. Press them down with your hand, just enough so they lie on the bottom of the pot.

Pour in just enough water to cover the plants (remember to measure it as you add it). You must

32

maintain the correct proportion of water to caustic soda (see the recipes). Be careful, and always wear gloves. When you are working with fragile leaves that require only minimal cooking, first pour in 5 to 10 quarts (5 to 10 liters) of water and bring it to a boil, and then immerse the plants. (Since the conversion from quarts to liters is less than a 10% difference, we've rounded the numbers; the actual conversion is 5.3 and 10.6 quarts).

Cooking

The cooking times listed in the recipes are as precise as possible, but they may vary slightly depending on the season in which the plants were picked. The hardier the fibers, the longer they will need to be cooked; however, the difference is only a matter of a few minutes. While you are an apprentice in papermaking, careful observation of the leaves' transformation is necessary.

It is very important to stir the mixture often. The fibers or leaves often get stuck together or compacted, causing the interior of the mass to be improperly cooked. Some very light plants form a sort of icecap that hides the large bubbles in the boiling water and can lead to the mixture overflowing the pot. Be careful when cooking and cleaning the leaves; boiling caustic soda is dangerous. Always wear gloves. Stirring often will allow you to survey the plants, get to know them, and observe their transformation.

Once you have mastered the basic cooking procedure, you will be encouraged to discover other plants to turn into paper, to enrich your aesthetic vocabulary. Don't forget that this book is primarily a starting point.

If you have to dispose of the cooking water outdoors, neutralize the solution with hydrochloric acid first. You can control this neutralization process with the help of litmus paper, available in pharmacies.

First rinse

After you strain the pulp comes the first rinse. It is important to remove all trace of caustic soda before chlorinating, or bleaching, the pulp, so rinse thoroughly. Only running water will do the trick, and do not forget to mix the fibers well under the water and spread them out often with your hands. The runoff water resulting from this rinse should be totally clear before bleaching.

Bleaching

In the recipes, I always advise using 9 fluid ounces (250 milliliters) of concentrated bleach for each discoloration; however, a basin of water with bleach can serve to discolor several successive plants. It's up to you to decide when the bleach solution is no longer effective. Stir well and constantly, first to ensure a homogeneous discoloration, and second, to maintain your vigilance. Being alert during this process will allow you to see and achieve the precise tonality that you want.

Don't be afraid to stop the bleaching process as often as necessary; this will let you achieve beautiful color gradations. But don't forget also that these colors resist the test of time in varying degrees. If you want real color, bleach the fibers and then dye them.

If you don't have time to use all the paper pulp that you have produced, freeze it, in small quantities, so you can use it easily later on.

Second rinse

You must be very meticulous with the second rinse, because the result of your paper depends on this stage. Eliminating all trace of the chlorine always seems impossible to me; but you must rinse it as much as possible.

After rinsing, your pulp should no longer smell of bleach. Note: your hands and your gloves, which have blended the pulp, will smell for a long time.

When you are pleased with the color of the pulp, rinse it quickly to stop the bleaching process. If you bleach the leaves in batches to achieve different tones of color, don't combine all the colors; have a basin in which to rinse each batch.

Creating the paper

1. Fill a basin 3/4 full of clear water—make sure that the basin is completely clean. Once you have made several sheets of paper, a bit of pulp will escape and cause the water to become slightly opaque. This doesn't matter in itself, but if, for example, you're working with a rather dark white oak leaf after having worked with bamboo, a film will attach to the oak and undermine the final result. Change the water in the basin often.

Make sure the mold and deckle fits into the basin well. You should be able to hold it comfortably without scraping your wrists against the sides of the basin. The mold and deckle consists of two frames: the mold is covered with netting and should always sit beneath the deckle—which will determine the shape and size of the paper—with the netting facing up, and not the opposite. Check the arrangement to avoid the mistake of placing them incorrectly.

The two frames should stack on top of one another perfectly.

Water is the miracle ingredient in paper-making, for the production of the pulp, but also for the realization of the sheets of paper. Always take this into account.

Your mold and deckle should rest in the water, but not too much. The netting should be totally submerged, but not the upper frame. Essentially, the ideal scenario is to always have the level of water hit halfway up the second frame. Maintaining the proper placement of the mold and deckle is difficult. Press it against the side of the basin in order to stabilize it.

Your fingers should firmly grasp the wood of the mold and deckle—only the wood, not the netting, with your wrists remaining supple.

Begin with an easy pulp: bamboo, giant reeds, or wild oat leaves. Take a small amount of pulp each time and spread it out on the mold and deckle.

2. Pat—don't rub—the pulp on the netting so it is uniformly dispersed and you will understand the "miraculous" quality of the water. The plant fibers arrange themselves and intermix.

3. A pretty sheet of paper must be even and have straight sides and perfect corners. When you master well-made sheets of paper, you can create anything you are capable of imagining. If the paper comes out irregularly, master its irregularity. Always keep your mold and deckle even and level. Your heart can be in the content of the work, but your head must always be concentrating on its form.

When you are satisfied with the paper, remove it from the water, keeping the mold and deckle horizontal. Delicately drain as much water off as possible.

4. Rest the mold and deckle on the side of the basin, grab its outer sides, and raise it vertically. If there are unruly fibers, leave them. With practice you will learn to avoid these.

5. Place a rag or cloth flat on a table and rest one side of the mold and deckle on the cloth. Position it carefully toward one end of the cloth so you can visualize where you would like the sheet of paper to end up. Rap the mold and deckle on the cloth with a strong, swift gesture and don't move it once you've placed it down or you might deform the sheet. Sponge off all the excess water, but don't rub the netting.

You can add to the paper by putting, for example, lace or fresh plants on the wet paper mold once you have placed it on the cloth. If you do, be aware that the paper will take longer to dry. If you remove the lace or plants at the last minute, the imprint will be perfect. If you remove them too soon, the imprint will be less striking and smoother.

4

5

6. Delicately lift the mold and deckle. If the paper adheres to it, sponge it off once more a bit, and lift it again. Remove the frame. Fold the sides of the cloth over the paper and place it gently over the plywood board or under the press, if you have one.

6

7. Place the clamp over the plywood board and tighten. Change the cloth two or three times, then put the paper on cardboard to dry. Change the cardboard until the paper is dry.

7

8. In the beginning, the paper will be very fragile, but as it begins to dry, it will resist handling and deformation better; therefore, adding details becomes harder to achieve. Be humble; nothing turns out perfectly the first

8

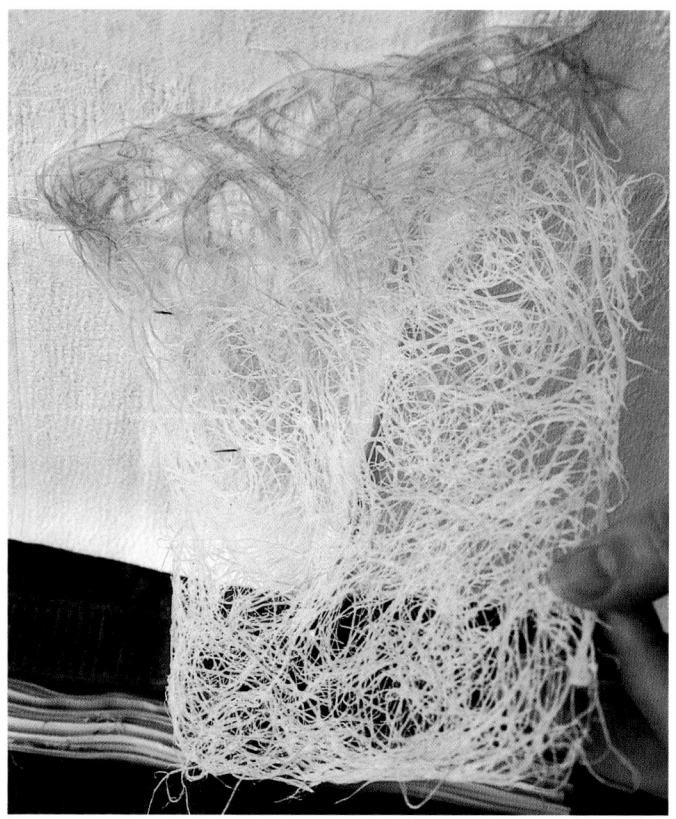

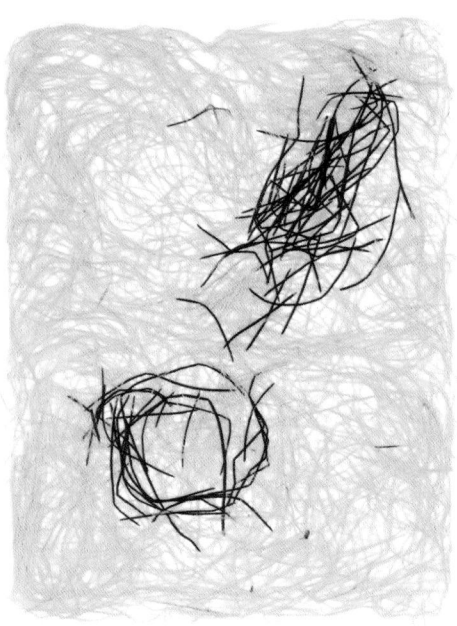

time around. Genius is rare, but with perseverance you can accomplish anything.

Sheets of paper are like mermaids—they develop all their charms in water. Outside of it, they can fold up into themselves. For example, take a chestnut leaf that you've turned into paper. Open it up and spread it out in water. Move the mold and deckle under the leaf and arrange it as you like. The leaf is dead, so you can tear, bend, or cut it to shape without a problem. Too much respect will harm it. That is, too much respect for the material will harm the creative endeavor.

Don't allow yourself to be locked in by the intrinsic beauty of the plants. They are the medium for your ideas, not the other way around.

If you tear a chestnut tree leaf down its middle, the central vein opens and breaks down into several fibers, several threads, both strong and fragile, like a scar.

If you bend the same leaf, each layer of thickness possesses its own graphic quality, its own color, adding, in a way, to all the others like transparent overlays. Remove the leaf from the water, strain it, and place it on a piece of cloth.

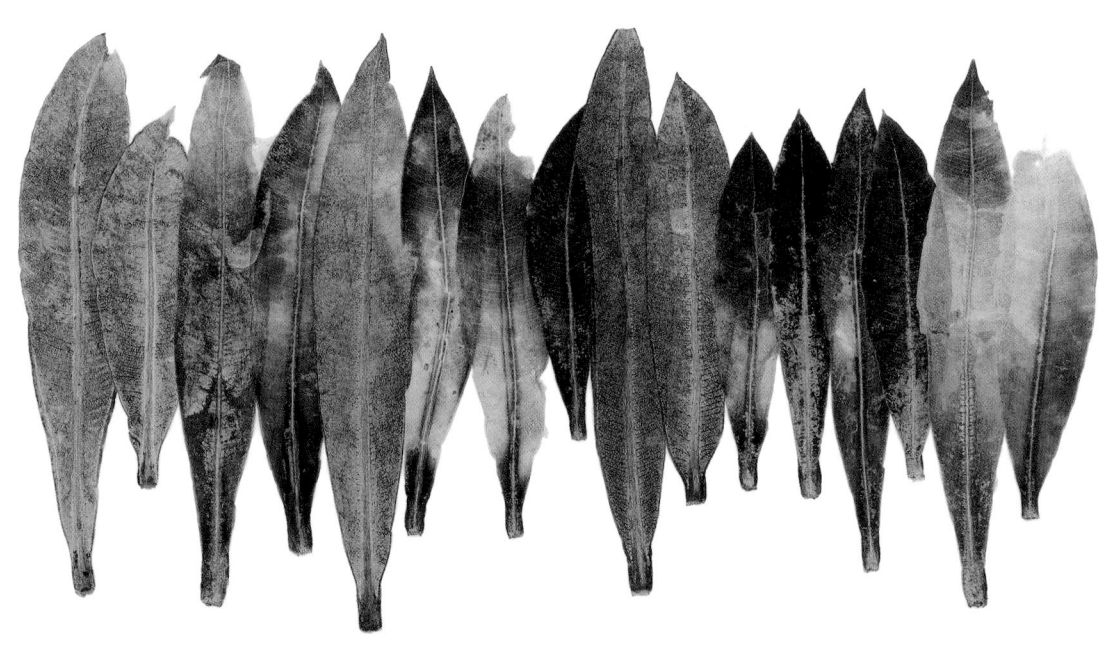

Recipes

Grasses

Bamboo
Wheat
Canna
Giant reed
Sedge plant (Carex)
Autumn crocus
Wild oat
Fern
Wild myrtle
Daylily
Pampas grass
Iris
Lavender
Cattail (Bulrush)
Spiderwort
Stinging nettle
Papyrus
Field horsetail
Yucca

Bamboo Paper

LOCATION
Grown in sunny areas with dry to moist soil; also in gardens.

HARVEST
Throughout the year. Cut only the stalks that carry the leaves.

PREPARATION
Cut the bamboo shoots. Put them in a pot and pour in 32 ounces (1 liter) of caustic soda per 10 quarts (10 liters) water.

COOK
One hour after it first comes to a boil. Stir often.

RINSE
Abundant and easy.

BLEACH
Pour 9 ounces (250 milliliters) of bleach in a basin of water. Stir the pulp well until it becomes a clear beige color.

RINSE
Abundant and easy.

RESULT
The pulp should be soft and fine.

USE
The paper is fragile but easy to write on.

FEEL
A very smooth paper. Remember that bamboo and blackberry bushes are materials widely used by wasps, the fathers of papermaking.

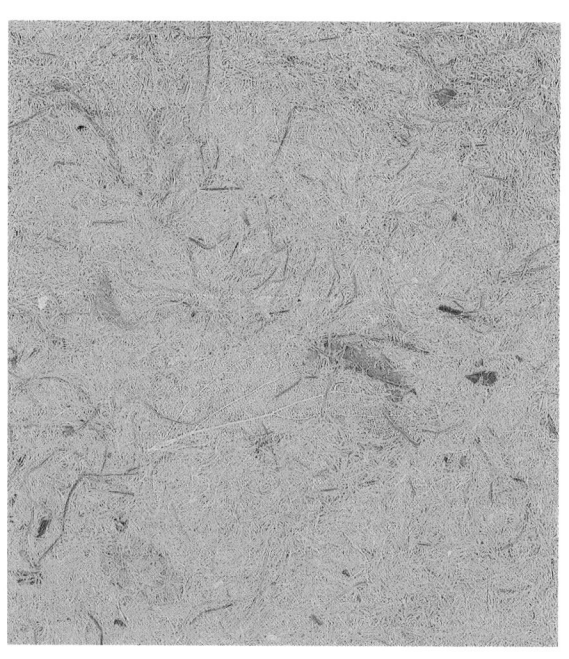
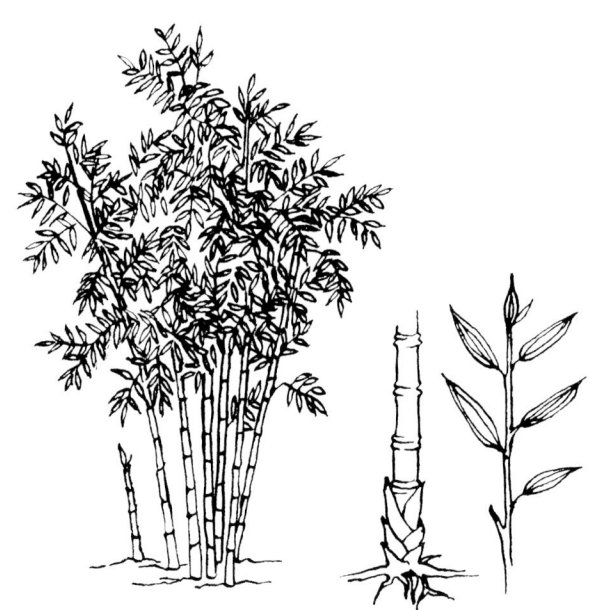

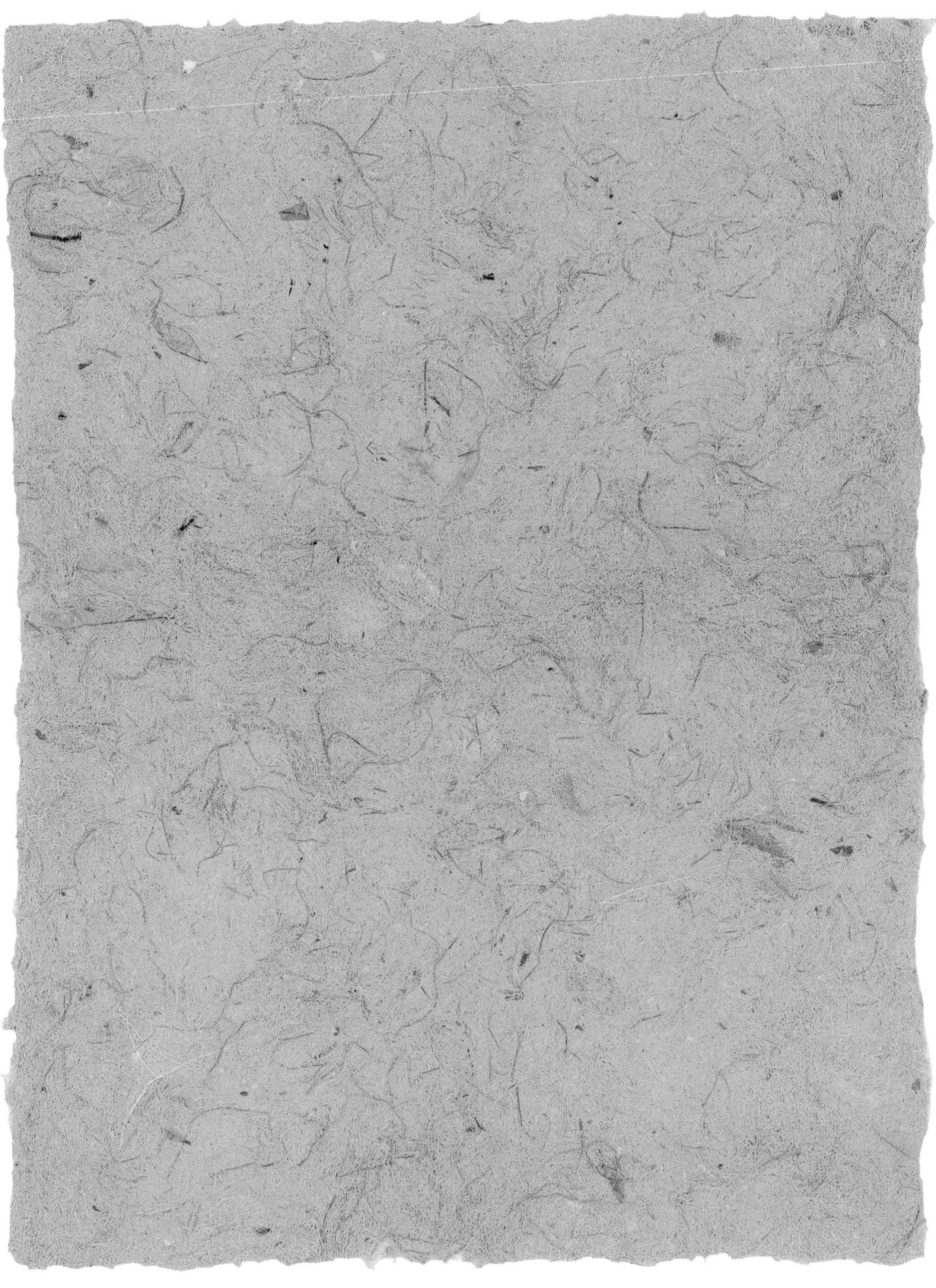

Wheat Paper

LOCATION
Found in fields.

HARVEST
At the maturity you choose. With permission of the proprietor, harvest the entire plant. Don't be greedy; wheat is plentiful and it is unnecessary to harvest more than you need. An armful is sufficient to make several dozen sheets of paper. If you do not know the field owner, a thatch, or similar grassy area of plant material, is also a good place to locate and gather wheat.

PREPARATION
Cut off and discard the roots. If you want to make cardboard instead of paper, keep the wheat grains. If not, remove them, but keep the ears; they give texture to the paper. Cut the plant into pieces approximately 10 to 12 inches (25 to 30 centimeters) long. Place them in a pot and pour in 32 ounces (1 liter) of caustic soda per 10 quarts (10 liters) of water.

COOK
Two hours after it first comes to a boil. Stir often and a lot, particularly if the stirring is difficult. The light mixture quickly forms into a sort of icecap; underneath, the stock bubbles rapidly.

RINSE
Abundant and painstaking, particularly if you have left the wheat grains in.

BLEACH
Pour 9 ounces (250 milliliters) of bleach in a basin of water. You can obtain a very mild white color, but stir conscientiously because the pulp is as compact as it is abundant.

RINSE
Abundant and meticulous

RESULT
A very pleasing pulp.

USE
This paper can be put to a number of uses, including writing. If you have made cardboard from the grains, you can mold the pulp into sculptures.

FEEL
A nearly ecstatic, rapturous feel, because with wheat you can do anything.

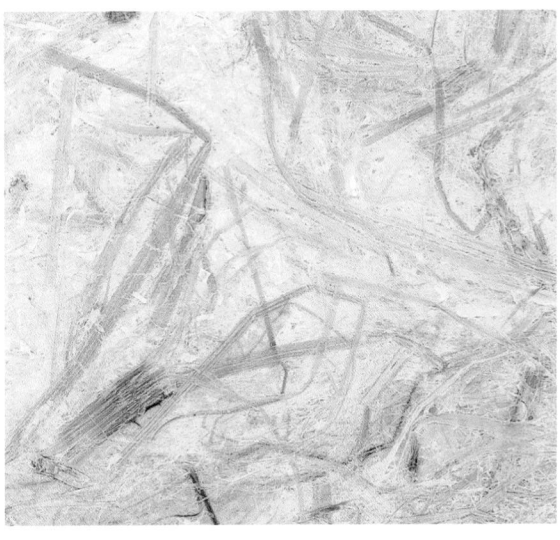

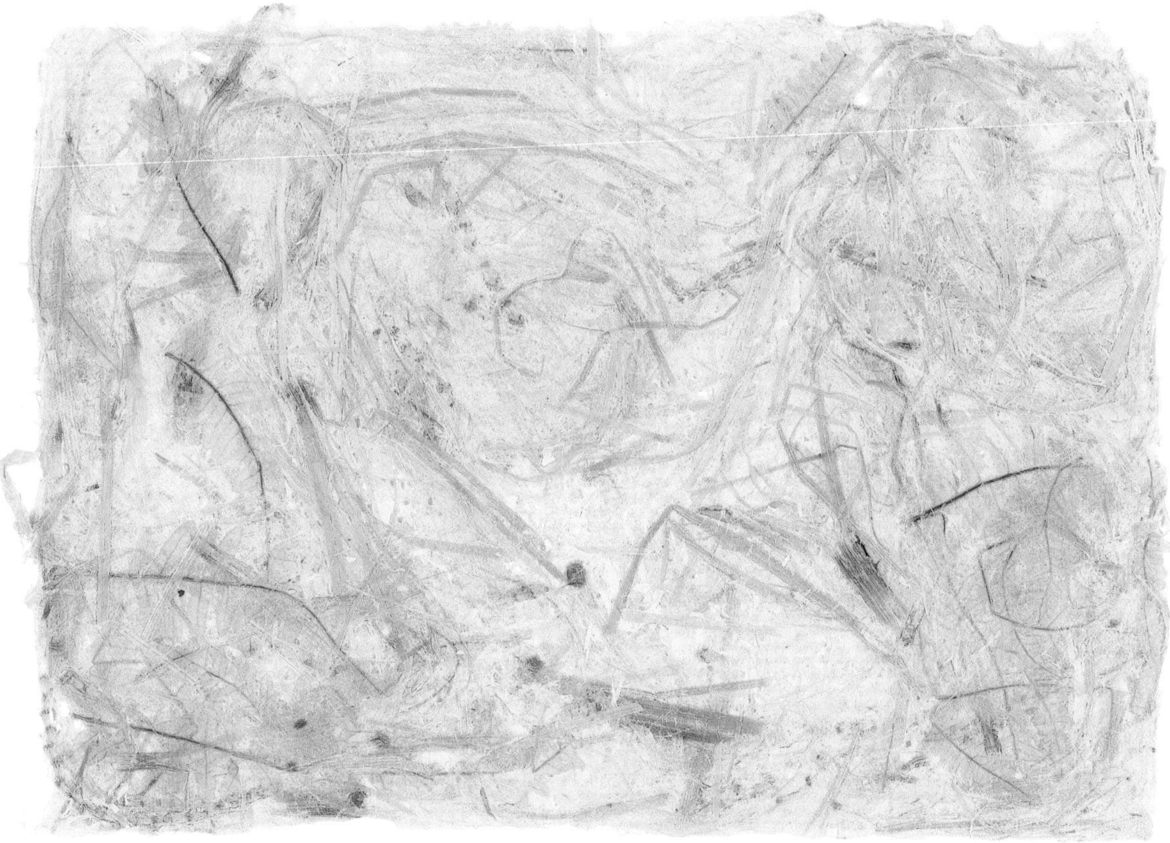

Wheat and chestnut paper

Canna Paper

LOCATION
Found in private or public gardens.

HARVEST
At the end of the season, cut the plant a few inches from the ground.

PREPARATION
Cut the stalks and the leaves into pieces approximately 10 to 12 inches (25 to 30 centimeters) long. Don't worry about the amount of leaves; they shrink down quickly. Put them in a pot and pour in 32 ounces (1 liter) of caustic soda per 10 quarts (10 liters) of water.

COOK
One hour and forty-five minutes after it first comes to a boil. Stir often.

RINSE
Abundant and easy, even though the pulp is very fine (it does not amount to much!).

BLEACH
Pour 9 ounces (250 milliliters) of bleach in a basin of water. Stir the pulp well. Be careful; if not, you won't have anything to rinse.

RINSE
Thoroughly and delicately, so as not to waste any.

RESULT
A fine, pleasing pulp.

USE
To demonstrate a miracle, even if it is small.

FEEL
To have produced a relic.

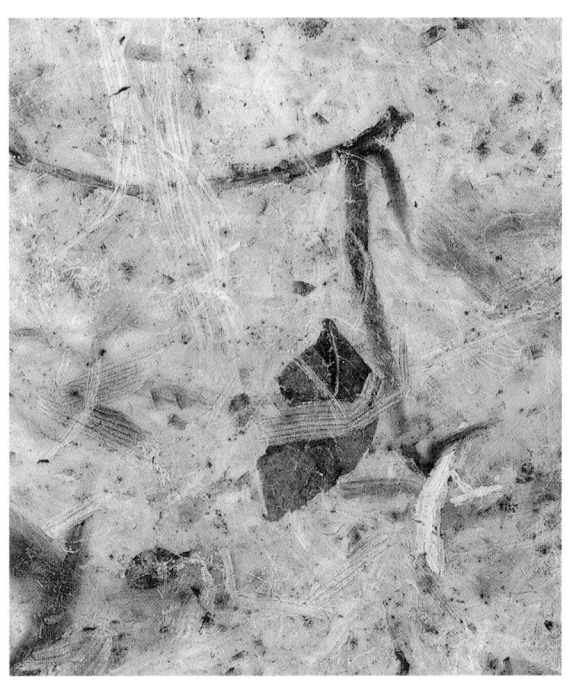

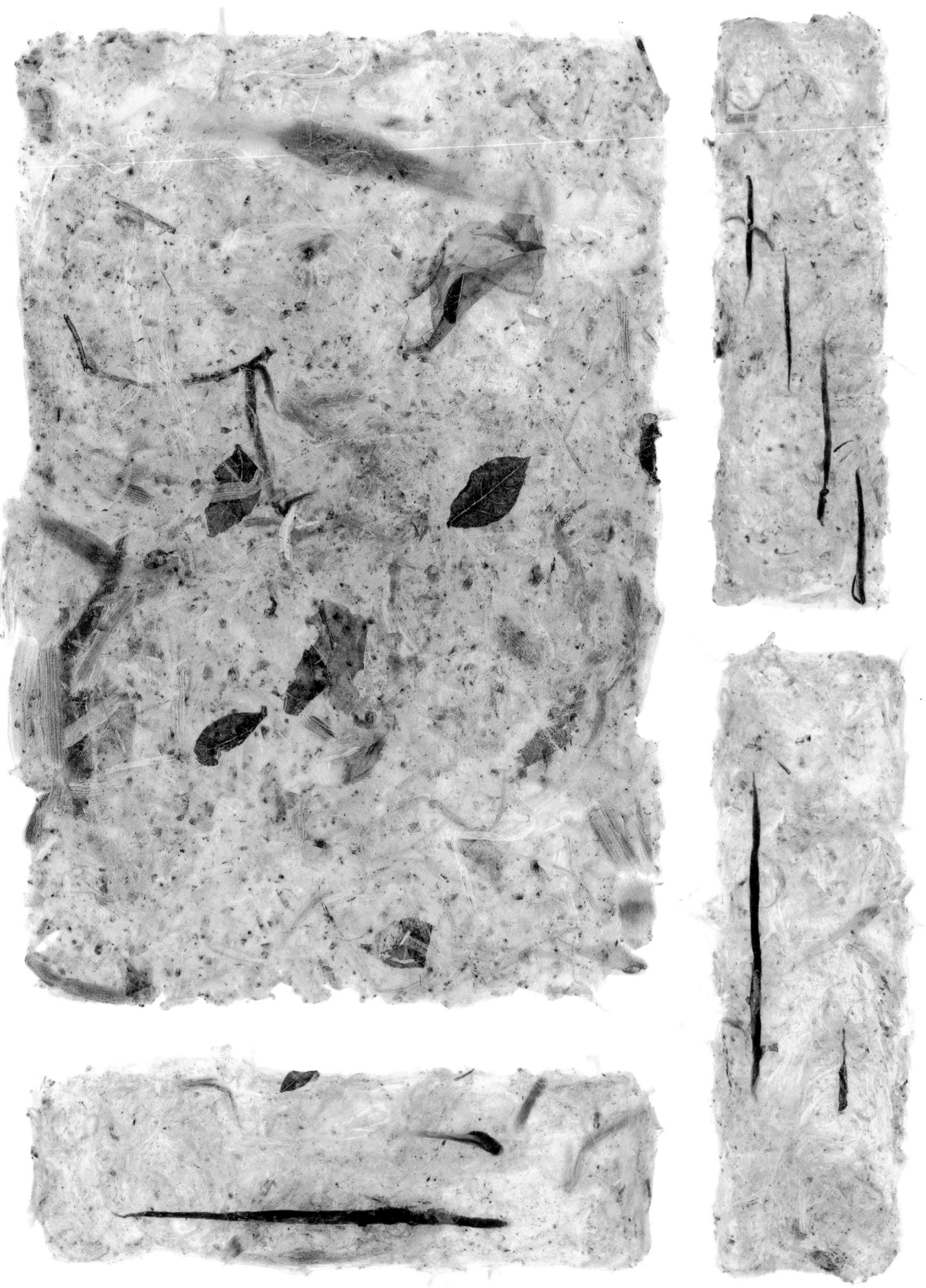

Giant Reed Paper

LOCATION
Found in humid, marshy regions. Often lining cultivated areas, reeds serve as hedges to block the wind.

HARVEST
In the summer months. Pick only the leaves.

PREPARATION
Cut the leaves in two. Place them in a pot and pour in 32 ounces (1 liter) of caustic soda per 10 quarts (10 liters) of water.

COOK
One hour after it first comes to a boil. Stir often.

RINSE
Abundant and easy.

BLEACH
Pour 9 ounces (250 milliliters) of bleach in a basin of water. Mix the pulp well, just until it becomes clear gray in color.

RINSE
Abundant and painstaking (after bleaching, the pulp becomes very fine).

RESULT
A soft, smooth pulp.

USE
Ideal for writing. The preparation is easy, and therefore perfect for beginners and children.

FEEL
Like a calm and mild dream.

Giant reed and bay leaf paper

Sedge Plant (Carex) Paper

LOCATION
Usually found along riverbanks, in ditches, marshes, and other warm, wet climates.

HARVEST
In season. Cut the leaves but do not pull up the roots.

PREPARATION
Cut the leaves in two. Put them in a pot and pour in 32 ounces (1 liter) of caustic soda per 10 quarts (10 liters) of water.

COOK
One hour and thirty minutes after it first comes to a boil. Stir often.

RINSE
Abundant and easy.

BLEACH
Pour 9 ounces (250 milliliters) of bleach in a basin of water. Mix the pulp well, just until it turns a clear gray color. The fibers are very fragile.

RINSE
Abundant and gentle.

RESULT
An exquisite, easy-to-use pulp.

USE
For writing.

Note: This paper pulp does not go very far, but, like paper made from giant reeds, it is very easy to use. Make the most of the pulp from the very beginning—be careful not to spill.

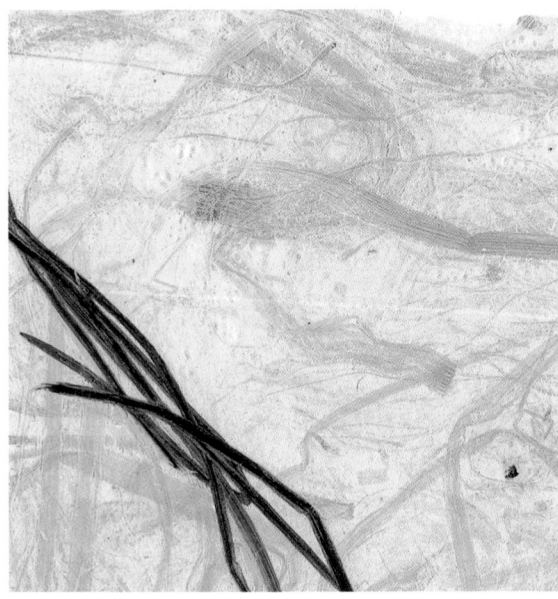
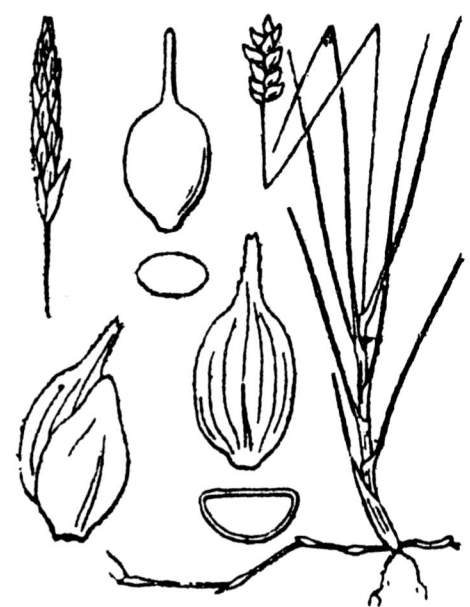

Sedge and pine needle paper

Autumn Crocus Paper

LOCATION
As a native to Europe and Asia, and as a naturalized plant in the United States, autumn crocus can be found in woodland areas, parks, and gardens.

HARVEST
In autumn, after the plant blossoms. Note: The bulbs need leaves in order to regenerate, so do not harvest the autumn crocus too early. Use the leaves that have fallen to the ground.

PREPARATION
Cut the leaves in two. Put them in a pot and pour in 32 ounces (1 liter) of caustic soda per 10 quarts (10 liters) of water.

COOK
One hour and thirty minutes after it first comes to a boil. Stir often.

RINSE
Abundant and meticulous. The pulp is compact and slightly viscous; separate the fibers well.

BLEACH
Pour 9 ounces (250 milliliters) of bleach in a basin of water. Mix the pulp well. You can achieve a very clear beige color, but the gradations of green in the beginning of the bleaching process are superb and resist the ravages of time and light well.

RINSE
Abundant and meticulous.

RESULT
A nearly transparent paper, similar to tracing paper. You can achieve perfectly straight edges and right angles.

USE
For writing; it also plays with and reflects light beautifully.

FEEL
A musical paper—soft and cold to the touch.

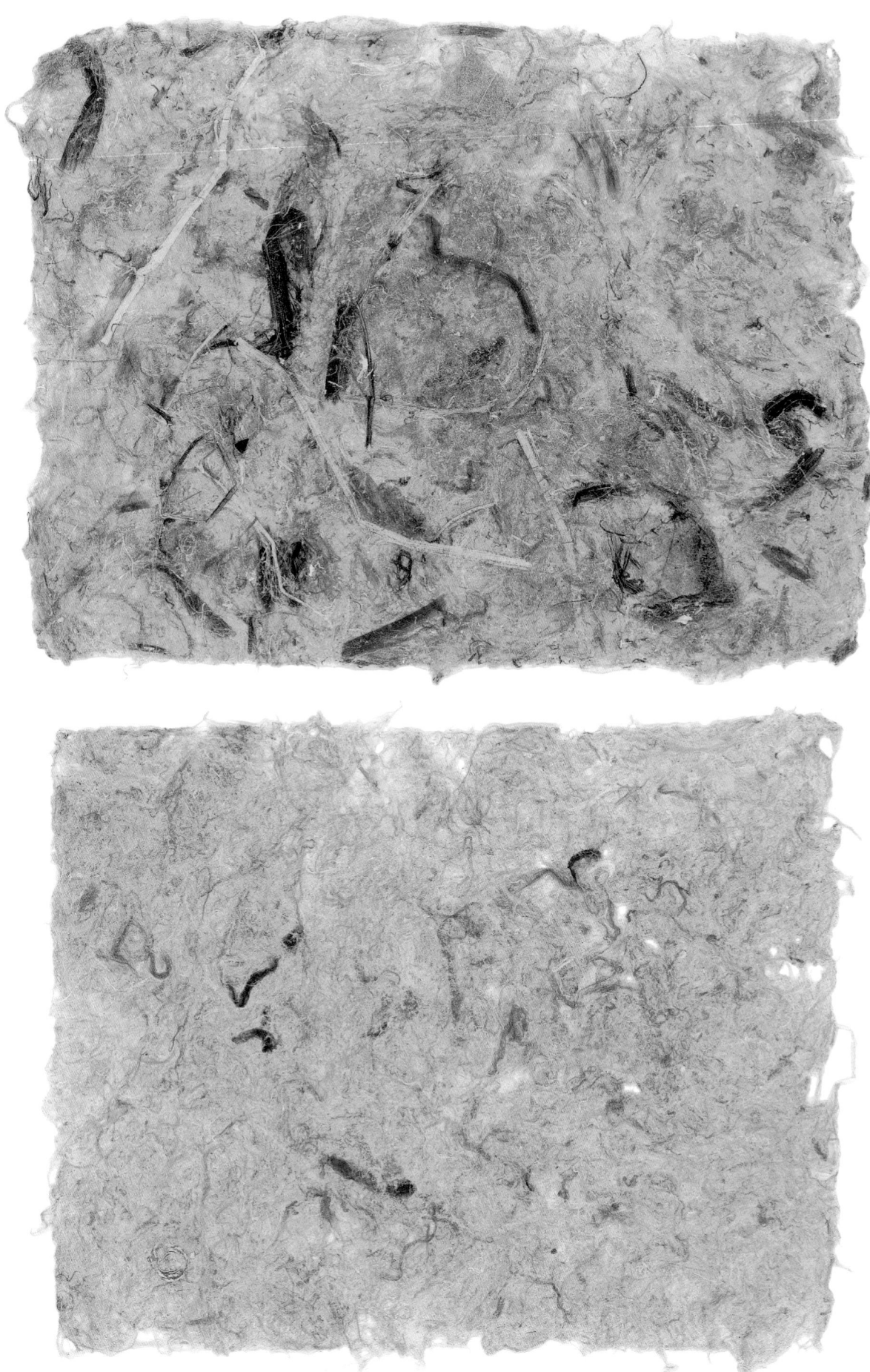

Wild Oat Paper

LOCATION
Found in uncultivated areas, along paths, or grown in woodland gardens.

HARVEST
The summer season.

PREPARATION
Use the entire plant except the roots. Cut it into pieces approximately 12 inches (30 centimeters) long. Put it all into a pot and pour in 32 ounces (1 liter) of caustic soda per 10 quarts (10 liters) of water.

COOK
Two hours after it first comes to a boil. Oats float for a long time, though you may not notice, and the water underneath boils very quickly. It can boil over easily. Stir often.

RINSE
Abundant and easy.

BLEACH
Pour 9 ounces (250 milliliters) of bleach in a basin of water. Mix the pulp conscientiously. You can achieve a very white pulp, but watch closely: there is a magical moment when the pulp is white but certain stems remain golden.

RINSE
Abundant and easy.

RESULT
A pulp that is fine and pleasant to touch.

USE
A substantial paper, perfect for writing. Because it holds together well, you can mold it to create sculptures.

FEEL
The soft strength is reassuring. Oats go a long way; they do not diminish much during cooking.

Wild oat leaf and chestnut paper

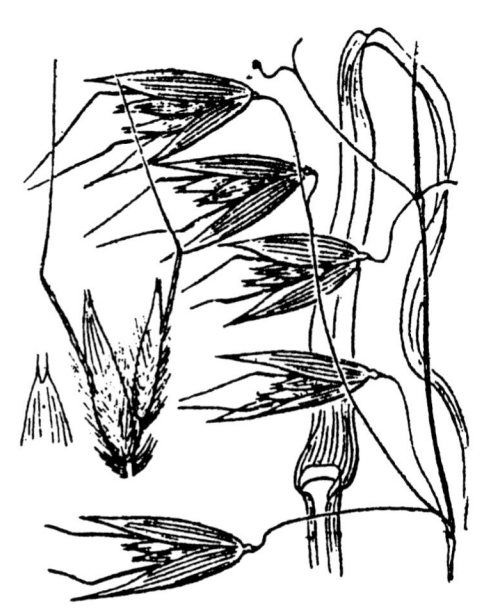

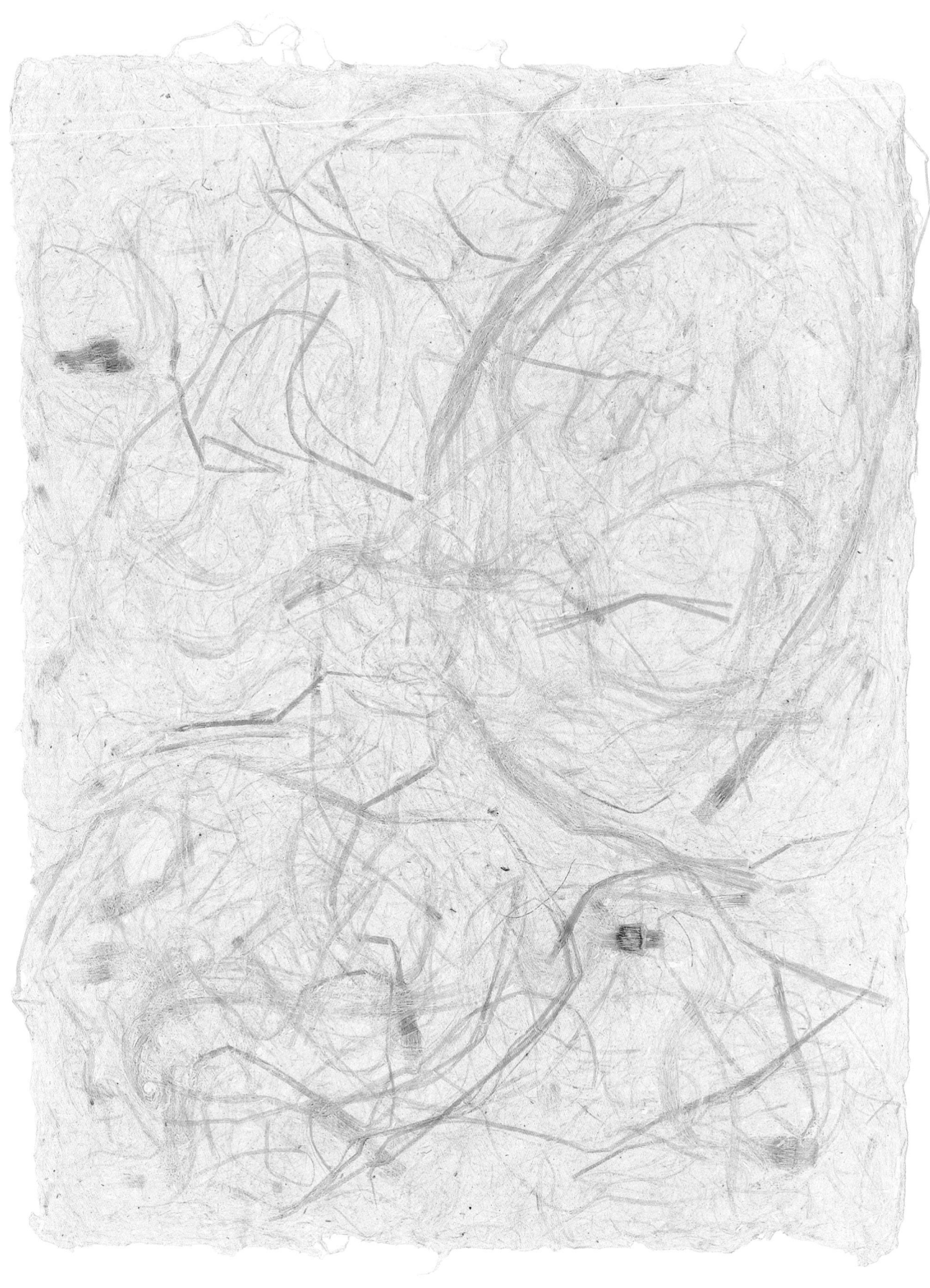

Fern Paper

LOCATION
Found in underbrush, woods, and gardens.

HARVEST
Remove all the large stems. Keep only the leaves. Put them in a pot and pour in 32 ounces (1 liter) of caustic soda per 10 quarts (10 liters) of water.

COOK
One hour and thirty minutes after it first boils. Stir often.

RINSE
Heavy, easy, and delicate, all at the same time.

BLEACH
Pour 9 ounces (250 milliliters) of bleach in a basin of water. Mix the leaves in well. The discoloration of the ferns is a wonder. After they cook, the leaves are brown, but very quickly they become gold, sun yellow, warm beige, clear beige, then transparent.

RINSE
Heavy, easy, and delicate.

RESULT
A very ornate paper, whether uniform in texture or not, of exquisite fineness.

USE
Light plays off this paper well. Ideal for enriching smoother, more compact, paper.

FEEL
A sense of fragility. A way of turning back time, when our planet did not yet know trees, much less human beings.

Wild Myrtle Paper

LOCATION
Widespread in woodland areas and along roadsides, especially in eastern and central United States.

HARVEST
In all seasons. Why not use your old, wilting flowers?

PREPARATION
Cut the leaves and the slim stalks; you may have to peel the fatter stalks (keep the peels for later use). Put them in a pot and pour in 32 ounces (1 liter) of caustic soda per 10 quarts (10 liters) of water.

COOK
Two hours after it first comes to a boil. Stir well.

RINSE
Abundant and easy. The pulp should remain fine.

BLEACH
Pour 9 ounces (250 milliliters) of bleach in a basin of water. Mix the pulp well. You can obtain a very white pulp with these strong, golden fibers.

RINSE
Abundant and gentle.

RESULT
A delicate pulp with some thicker, rigid fibers.

USE
Only fine pulp lends itself well to writing paper. Thicker fibers result in lovely details. The two, when combined, result in a strong, solid paper that is well-suited to sculpture.

FEEL
A little rough on the surface but very soft otherwise.

Note: If you want to create a paper of supple lace, cook the peels separately.

Daylily Paper

LOCATION
Cultivated in parks and gardens. Also found growing wild along roadsides and woodland areas in southern and midwestern United States and Europe.

HARVEST
After blossoming.

PREPARATION
Cut the leaves and stems in two. Put them in a pot and pour in 32 ounces (1 liter) of caustic soda per 10 quarts (10 liters) of water.

COOK
Two hours after it first comes to a boil. Stir often.

RINSE
Abundant and easy.

BLEACH
Pour 9 ounces (250 milliliters) of bleach in a basin of water. Mix the pulp well.

RINSE
Abundant and easy.

RESULT
A smooth, soft pulp, easy to work with.

USE
Writing paper, a little translucent.

Note: A pleasant surprise: after cooking, the fibers are nearly black; during bleaching, they become as orange as the flowers they carry in the spring, but this color does not last long. Watch the bleaching process closely.

Pampas Grass Paper

LOCATION
Abundant in coastal zones; a fine display found on the California coast, in parks, and in gardens.

HARVEST
All year long. Select leaves of your preference and cut them from the bottom of the plant to avoid damaging the plant itself. Attention: The leaves are razor-sharp; be sure to wear gloves.

PREPARATION
Cut the leaves into pieces approximately 10 inches (20 centimeters) long. Put them in a pot and pour in 32 ounces (1 liter) of caustic soda per 10 quarts (10 liters) of water.

COOK
Two hours after it first comes to a boil. Stir often.

RINSE
Abundant and easy.

BLEACH
Pour 9 ounces (250 milliliters) of bleach in a basin of water. Mix the pulp well. You can obtain white fibers, but before you do you will see a range of colors, from green to yellow, passing through the most lively orange.

RINSE
Abundant and easy.

RESULT
Very solid, non-pulpy fibers, except perhaps the whitest, which are a little less hardy because of the bleaching.

USE
This paper is favorable to the addition of very exquisite and strong details.

FEEL
Surprisingly solid and delicate.

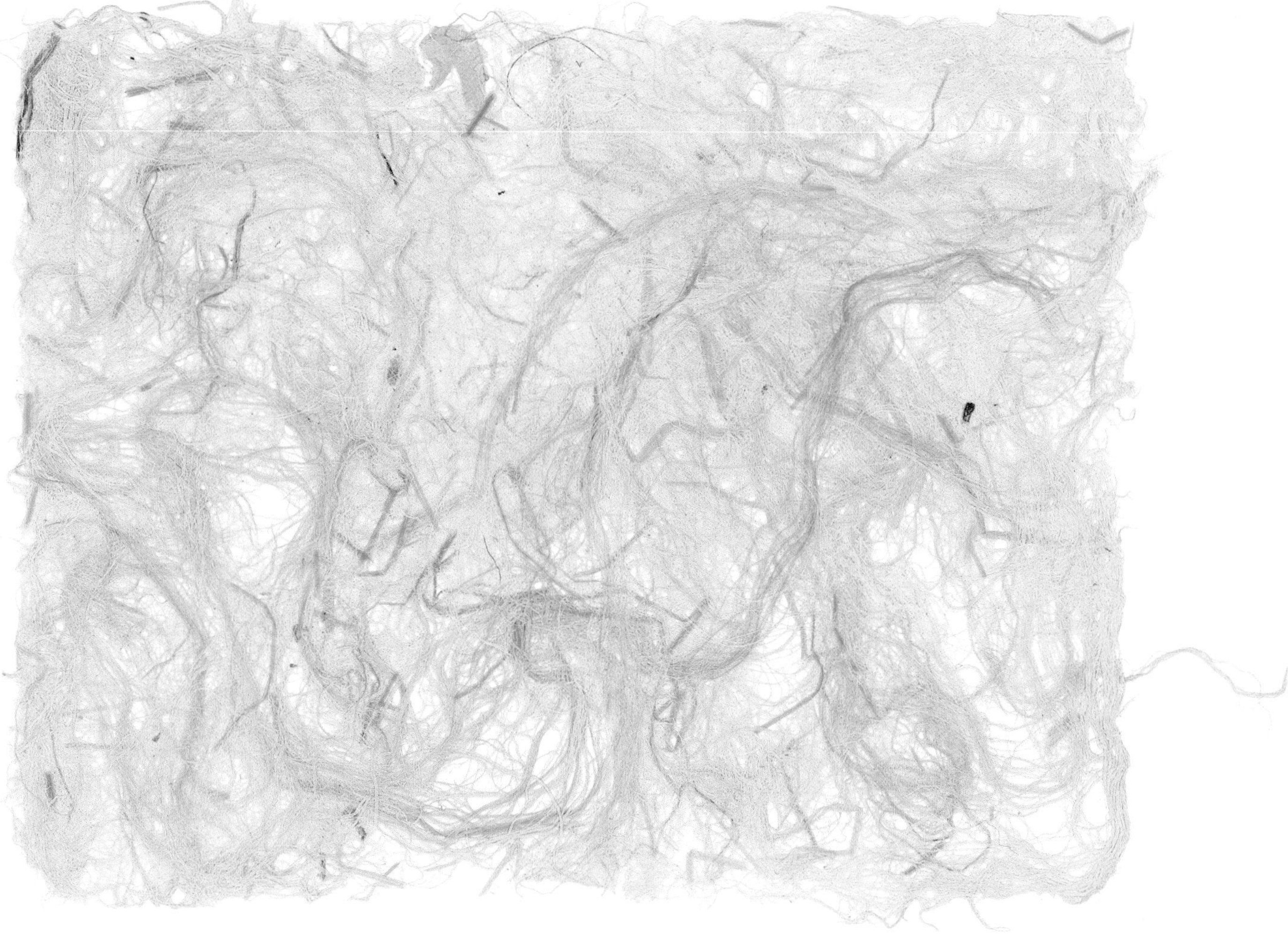

Pampas grass and pine needle paper

Iris Paper

LOCATION
Found in gardens. Here and there, in nature. All varieties of iris are well suited to paper production.

HARVEST
At the end of the season. Cut the leaves about 4 inches (10 centimeters) from the ground. At the end of the plant the leaves tend to be dry; tear them off, as well as any rotten stems.

PREPARATION
Cut the leaves and stems into pieces about 10 to 12 inches (25 to 30 centimeters) long. Put them in a pot and pour in 32 ounces (1 liter) of caustic soda per 10 quarts (10 liters) of water.

COOK
Two hours after it first comes to a boil. Stir often.

RINSE
Abundant and easy.

BLEACH
Pour 9 ounces (250 milliliters) of bleach in a basin of water. Mix well. Irises are very fibrous and the pulp thickens quickly; the center of this large mass of pulp often remains green. Stir until it becomes nearly completely white, but the beginning of the bleaching process is often very beautiful (the shades of green and brown are very subtle).

RINSE
Abundant and easy.

RESULT
You will obtain a small amount of fine pulp with long, solid fibers.

USE
For writing and sculpting.

FEEL
The fibers are rippled, light, and some are brilliantly iridescent. The swirling textures are poignant. If you do not use the pulp to make paper, you can create iris lace that weighs next to nothing.

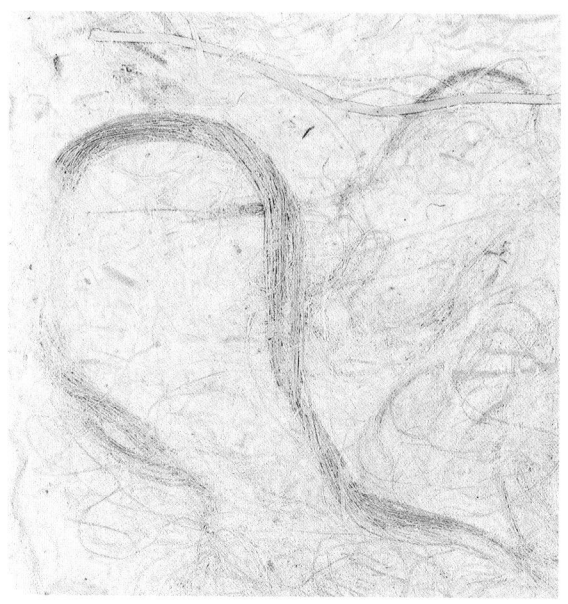

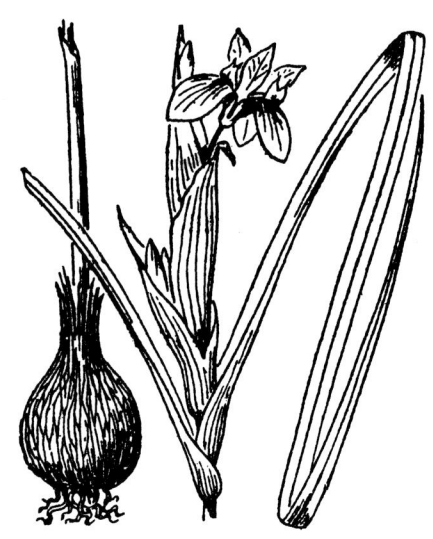

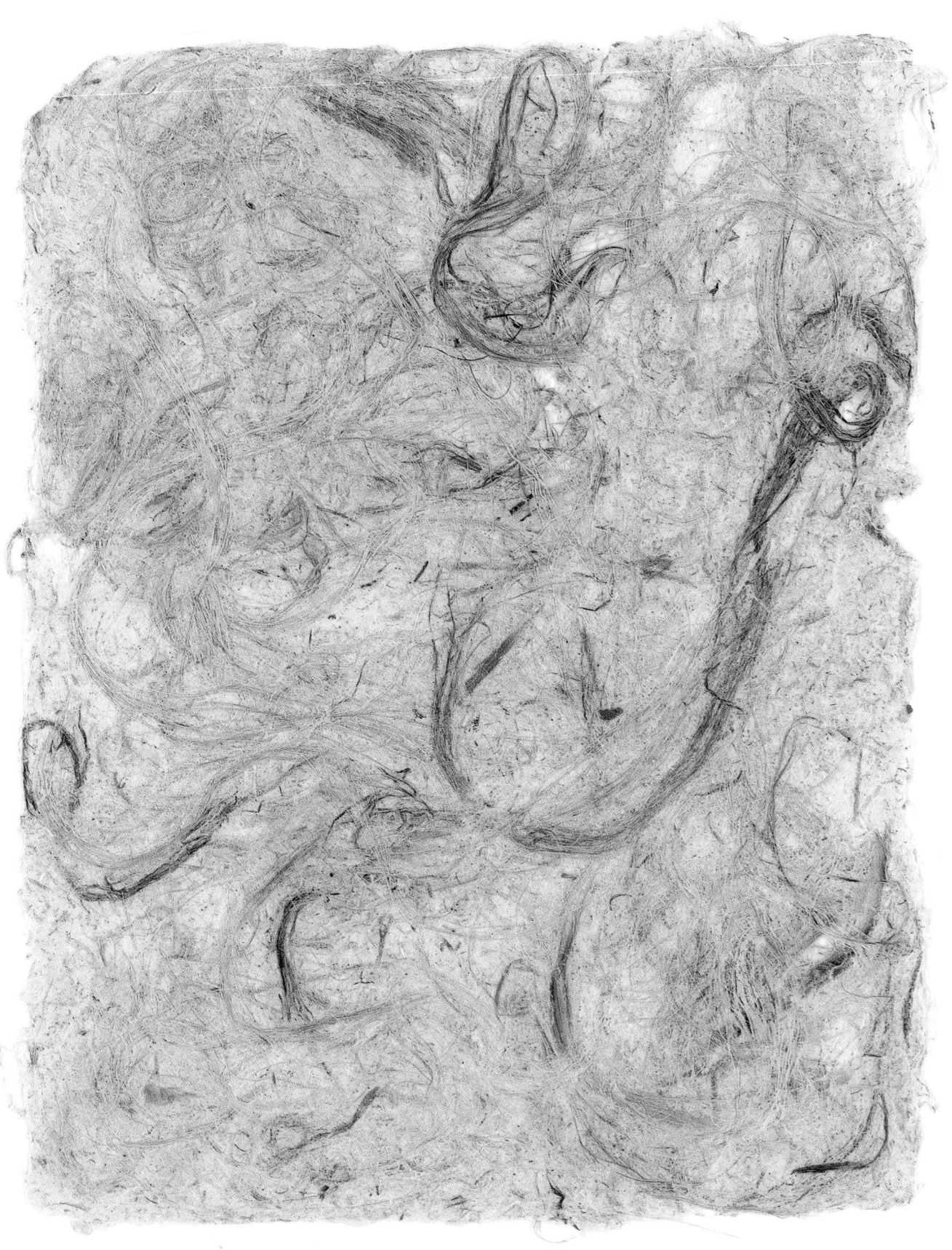

Lavender Paper

LOCATION
In gardens and dry scrublands.

HARVEST
Anytime after blossoming. Harvest the stems and wilted ears. Handle the plant carefully.

PREPARATION
Cut the stems in two. Put them in a pot and pour in 32 ounces (1 liter) of caustic soda per 10 quarts (10 liters) of water.

COOK
Two hours after it first comes to a boil. Stir often.

RINSE
Abundant and easy.

BLEACH
Pour 9 ounces (250 milliliters) of bleach in a basin of water. Mix the pulp well. You can obtain a nearly white pulp.

RINSE
Abundant and easy.

RESULT
You will have practically no fine pulp, but fibers ragged down to their ends.

USE
A true godsend to convey anger: create paper of great character, or even sculptures.

FEEL
The fibers remain soft. A nice paradox: visually, the fibers are straight and ragged-looking, but they are soft to the touch. C'est la vie.

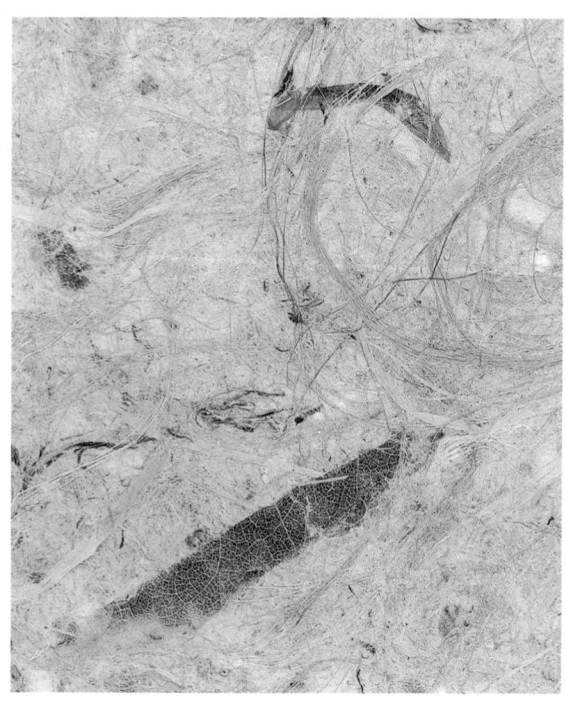

Cattail (Bulrush) Paper

LOCATION
Found in widespread areas on the edges of marshes.

HARVEST
In the summer, cut them 4 inches (10 centimeters) from the ground.

PREPARATION
Cut the plant into pieces 10 to 12 inches long (25 to 30 centimeters). Put them all in a pot and pour in 32 ounces (1 liter) of caustic soda per 10 quarts (10 liters) of water.

COOK
Two hours after it first comes to a boil.

RINSE
Copious and meticulous. The fibers pack together quickly.

BLEACH
Pour 9 ounces (250 milliliters) of bleach in a basin of water. Combine the pulp well. You can achieve a lovely white, but the beige-gray gradations are magnificent.

RINSE
Abundant and meticulous.

RESULT
A paper that expresses itself with depth. Its spiral fibers are superb—do not deprive yourself of them. Mix the colors well.

USE
Though it is easily written on, you might hesitate to do so because it is so beautiful.

FEEL
Not of paper, but a caress, soft and warm. Indispensable.

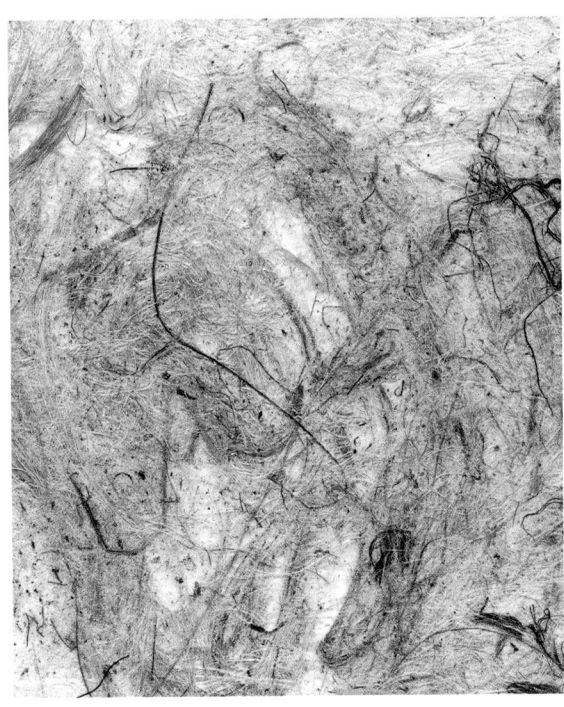
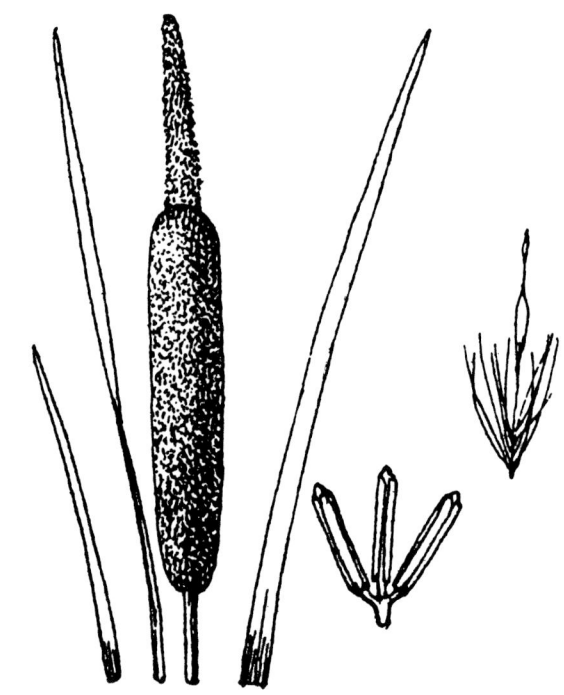

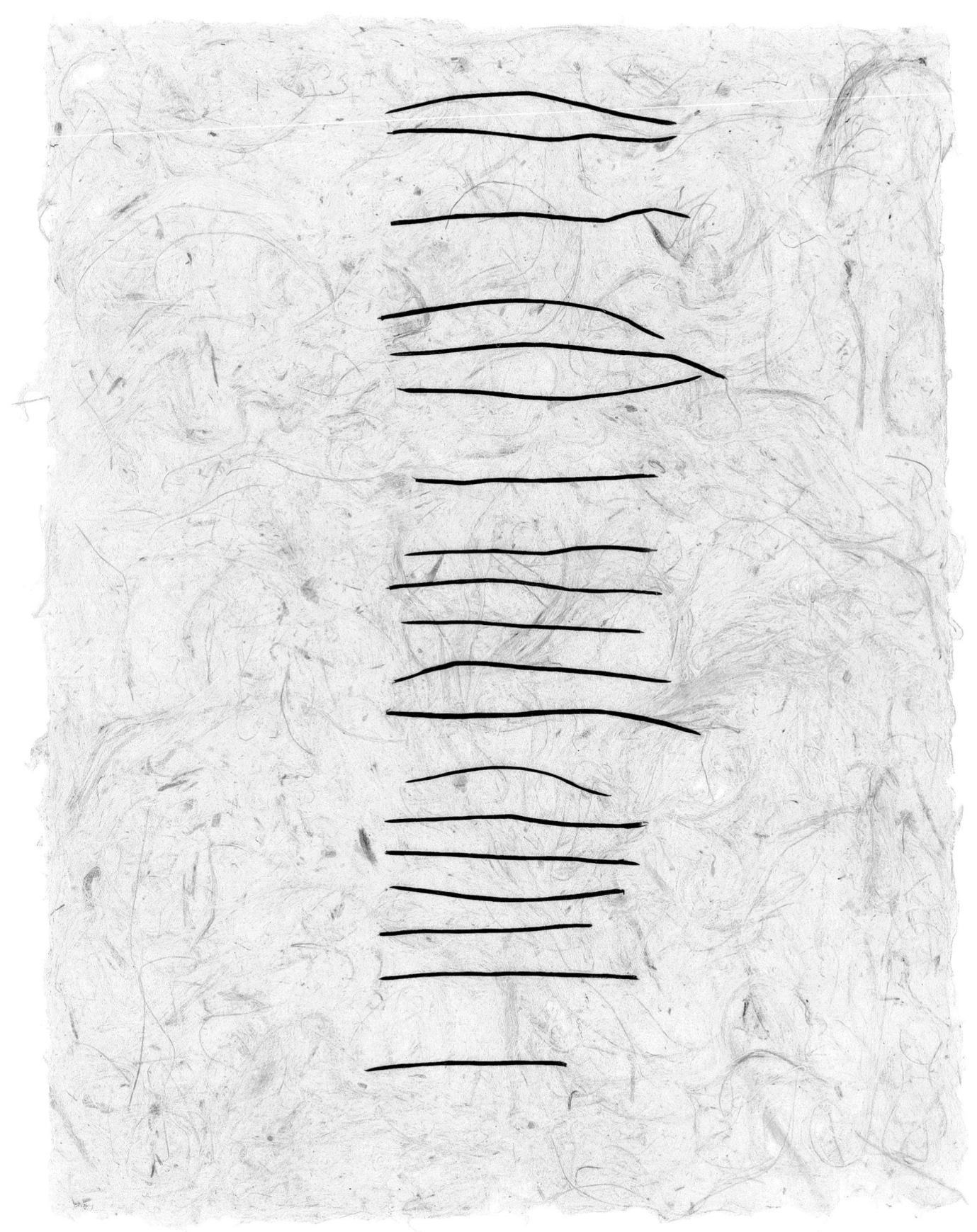

Cattail and pine needle paper

Spiderwort Paper

LOCATION
Found in moist areas on sandy, rocky, or clayey soil, along roadsides, railroads, on prairies, and in open woodlands. Also cultivated in gardens.

HARVEST
The summer season. Gather the entire plant except the roots.

PREPARATION
Put everything in a pot and pour in 32 ounces (1 liter) of caustic soda per 10 quarts (10 liters) of water.

COOK
One hour after it first comes to a boil. Stir gently. Closely watch the cooking process and the disintegration of the material.

RINSE
Copious and delicate. Don't waste any of the little material that remains.

BLEACH
Pour 9 ounces (250 milliliters) of bleach in a basin of water. Mix the pulp gently. The process is delicate, be careful. Don't go beyond achieving a beige or clear green color.

RINSE
Abundant and delicate.

RESULT
A fine pulp with some thicker portions (from the small rings that segment the stalk).

USE
A compact base on which to write or paint. The pulp does not go very far, but it is useful for its symbolic qualities.

FEEL
Soft. A soulful pleasure.

Note: Do not be concerned by how little pulp this plant creates. Spiderwort is filled with water. Remember that sometimes the process is more important than the result. In the end, when you handle what is left of the cooked plant, it nearly disappears. More or less reassuring, isn't it?

Stinging Nettle Paper

LOCATION
Widespread. Found growing in the country-side, gardens, sandy fields, and rocky areas—prolific in the western United States and throughout the United Kingdom and the rest of Europe.

HARVEST
Throughout the summer season. Choose the largest and fattest stinging nettle plants. Pick the entire plant except the roots. Even in the summer, cover yourself entirely before gathering and preparing nettles. Wear gloves.

PREPARATION
Remove the leaves and cut the stems slightly shorter than the diameter of your pot. Put it all in a pot and pour in 32 ounces (1 liter) of caustic soda per 10 quarts (10 liters) of water.

COOK
Two hours after it first comes to a boil. Stir often.

RINSE
Abundant and easy. When the water is completely clear, take each piece of stem between your thumb and index finger, press, and tear from the top towards the bottom to remove all the silk threads. Each time you do this you will remove more and more. The most beautiful papers require the most work, and the patience of an angel.

BLEACH
Pour 9 ounces (250 milliliters) of bleach in a basin of water. Mix the stinging nettle silk well and stir just until it turns completely white.

RINSE
Abundant and gentle.

RESULT
Stinging nettle silk is wonderfully soft. You can develop undulations and slight differences in thickness in the pulp.

USE
A paper perfect for spicy, even biting love letters.

FEEL
A delight to touch, to view its spirit. What could be more lovely than the worst of weeds turning into the most beautiful of papers? It reconciles you with the entire earth.

Stinging nettle and leftover deposits of cooked leaves

Papyrus Paper

LOCATION
Though native to Egypt and tropical Africa, papyrus is cultivated in warm, humid regions.

HARVEST
Use the entire papyrus plant. Harvest it in the summer when the plant is blossoming. Cut the plant 4 inches (10 centimeters) from the ground.

PREPARATION
Cut into pieces approximately 9 inches (23 centimeters) long. Use the flowered head. Put everything in a pot and pour in 32 ounces (1 liter) caustic soda per 10 quarts (10 liters) of water.

COOK
Two hours after it first comes to a boil. Stir often—the heads of the flower float for a long time.

RINSE
Abundant and easy. Note: In the middle of the fine, long fibers there are small grains, like an infinite number of punctuation marks. A unique treasure.

BLEACH
Pour 9 ounces (250 milliliters) of bleach in a basin of water. Delicately mix the pulp. Be careful: Recognize that you are working with an exceptional material. Do not go beyond achieving a clear beige color, but before you do, the brown gradations are very beautiful.

RINSE
Abundant, easy, and meticulous.

RESULT
This is a paper on which to write, tell stories, and offer a nod to our Egyptian friends who used a variety of this very papyrus to produce the forerunner of paper.

FEEL
A soft, light paper with a scent of eternity.

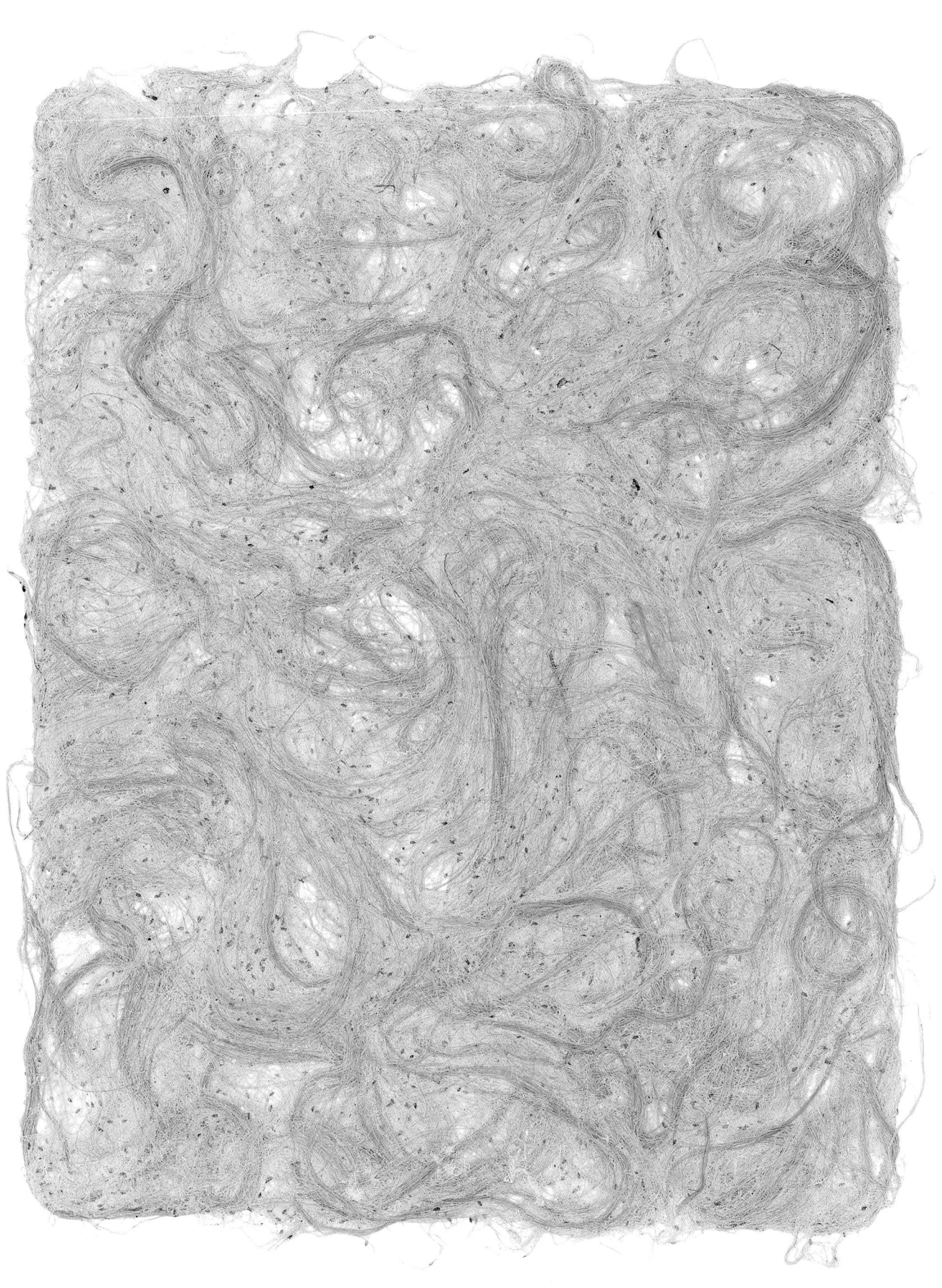

Field Horsetail Paper

LOCATION
Widespread; found in humid areas, often growing on the edges of ponds.

HARVEST
In the summer, cut the entire plant 4 inches (10 centimeters) from the ground.

PREPARATION
It is unnecessary to cut the horsetails again. Put them in a pot and pour in 32 ounces (1 liter) of caustic soda per 10 quarts (10 liters) of water.

COOK
Two hours after it first comes to a boil. Stir often.

RINSE
Abundant and easy.

BLEACH
Pour 9 ounces (250 milliliters) of bleach in a basin of water. Mix the pulp well. It will almost completely lose its color.

RINSE
Abundant and easy.

RESULT
The stems consist of a series of very beautiful, brown rings; the underside of each ring remains very dark, almost black.

USE
This is a very fine paper. The stems have a very Japanese look to them. You may place all the pulp in a mixer to achieve a more compact result.

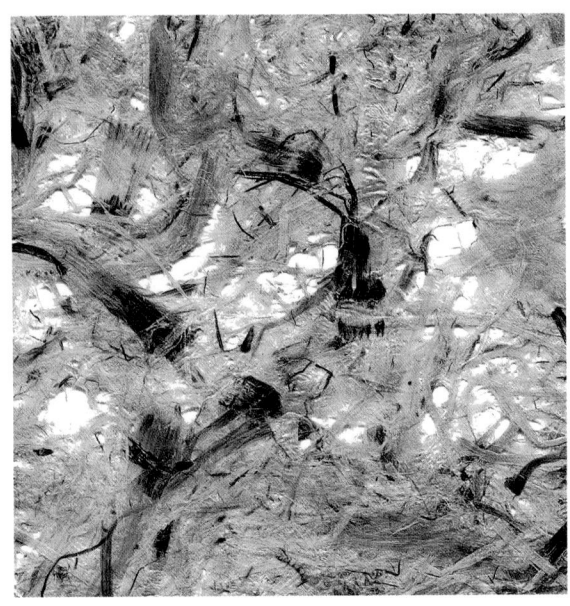

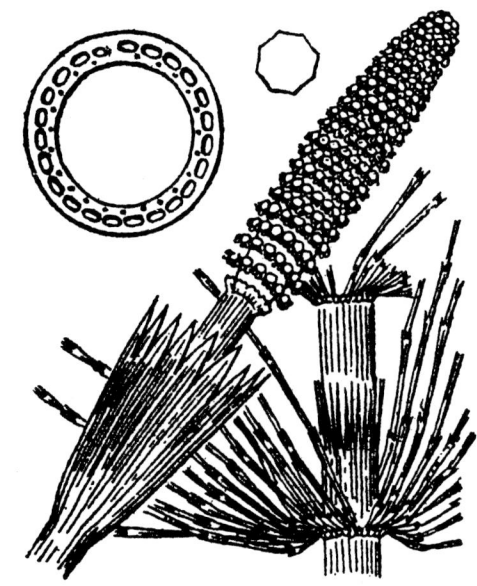

Yucca Paper

LOCATION
Found in dry, sandy areas near coastal dunes. Also cultivated in parks and gardens.

HARVEST
Throughout the year. Select from the dried leaves that accumulate at the foot of the plant.

PREPARATION
If you use fresh leaves; let them dry; if you do not, foam will quickly form during the cooking process, causing the mixture to overflow. Cut the leaves into pieces 10 to 12 inches (25 to 30 centimeters) long. Put them in a pot and pour in 1.5 quarts (1.5 liters) of caustic soda per 10 quarts (10 liters) of water.

COOK
Two hours and thirty minutes after it first comes to a boil. Stir often.

RINSE
Abundant and meticulous. Spread the fibers apart well; they have a tendency to stick together.

BLEACH
Pour 9 ounces (250 milliliters) of bleach in a basin of water. Mix the pulp well. You can mix until you achieve white, but certain tones of brown and yellow are superb.

RINSE
Abundant and meticulous.

RESULT
The fibers are extraordinarily strong, even the most bleached.

USE
The firmness of these fibers allows for the creation of impressive sculptures, fine lace, or light, threadlike strands.

FEEL
A little rough, as in nature. Yucca lace doesn't weigh anything and is very strong. Miraculously, it is as light as air.

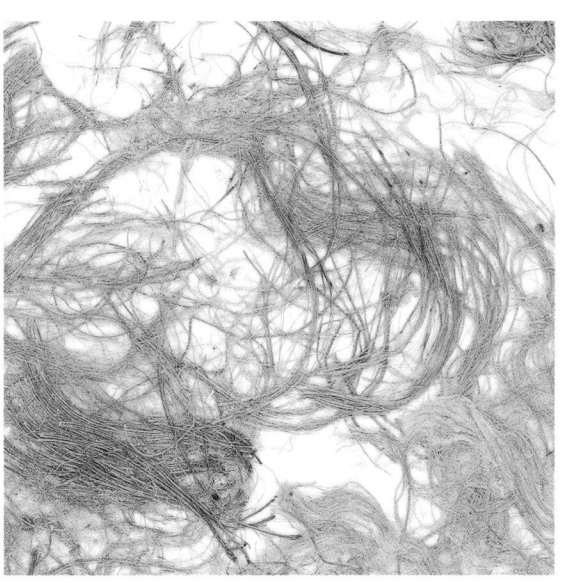

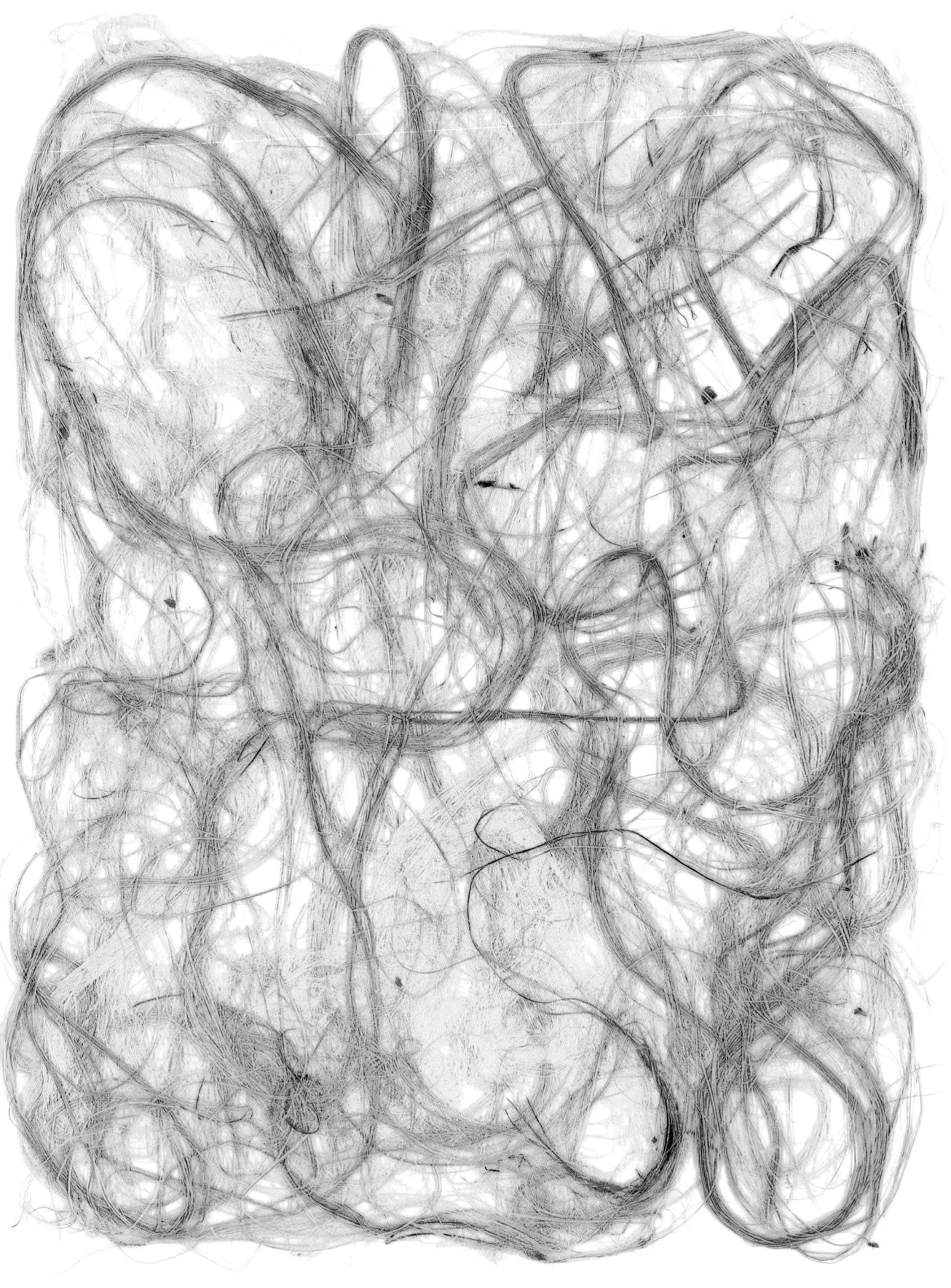

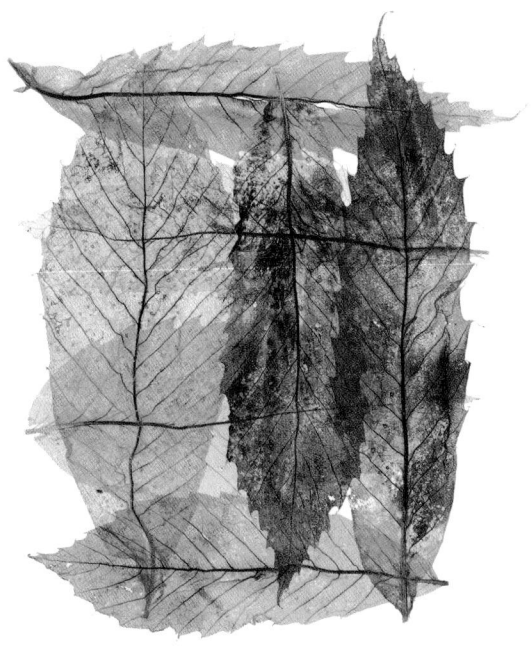

Trees

Hornbeam
Chestnut
White oak
Holm oak
Montpellier maple
Ginkgo biloba
Oleander
Elm
Blackberry bush
Wild olive
Palm
Poplar
Pine
Pistachio
Lime

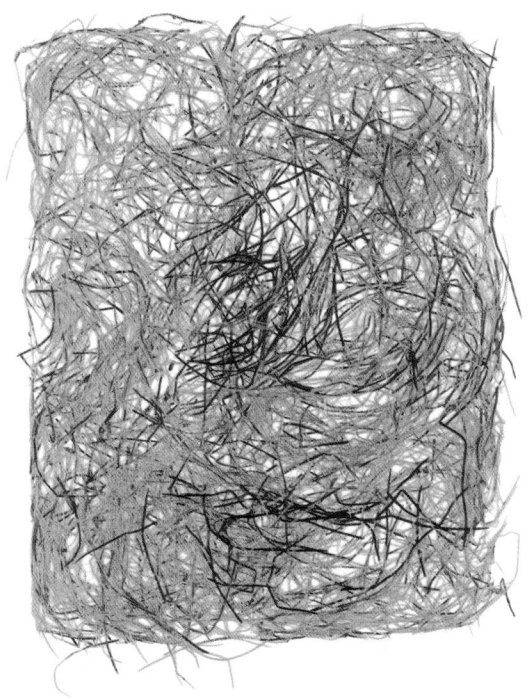

Hornbeam Paper

LOCATION
Found in forests, swamps, along rivers, streams, and streets, and in parks, woodlands, and gardens.

HARVEST
At the end of the season, but before the leaves fall. Cut the leaves, not the branches.

PREPARATION
Put the leaves in a pot and pour in 32 ounces (1 liter) of caustic soda per 10 quarts (10 liters) of water.

COOK
Put the leaves in only after the water first comes to a boil, and do not let them cook longer than one hour.

RINSE
Abundant and easy. Do not place the leaves directly under the spout, because the rush of water may damage them.

BLEACH
Pour 9 ounces (250 milliliters) of bleach in a basin of water. Mix the leaves well, but gently. They are extremely fine and fragile; do not let them sit in the bleach for too long.

RINSE
Abundant and easy.

RESULT
A small miracle: the leaves remain whole and green, as in nature, yet have a rather transparent, disembodied look.

USE
All sorts of work requires the use of plant material, but this is lighter than the blow of a kiss to a baby.

FEEL
An incomparable touch; finer than silk.

Chestnut Paper

LOCATION
Once prolific in forests of the eastern United States, a blight killed off nearly every chestnut tree by 1940. Some trees can still be found in cool, sandy regions, up to 2,640 feet (800 meters) in altitude, and in woodlands, gardens, and along roadsides throughout Europe. The Chinese chestnut is often grown as a substitute in the United States.

HARVEST
During the summer season. Cut the leaves, not the branches; don't forget that they carry fruit.

PREPARATION
Put the leaves in a pot and pour in 32 ounces (1 liter) of caustic soda per 10 quarts (10 liters) of water.

COOK
One hour and thirty minutes after it first comes to a boil. Stir often and gently to avoid damaging the leaves.

RINSE
Abundant and easy.

BLEACH
Pour 9 ounces (250 milliliters) of bleach in a basin of water. Gently mix the leaves. You can achieve totally transparent leaves, revealing only their skeletons. But note: All the color gradations are superb. You will notice extraordinarily luminous browns and yellows.

Take advantage of this and stop the bleaching process as often as you want. You can obtain interesting color gradations by placing very little water in the basin and mixing forcefully (contrary to the usual rule). The bleaching effect in this case is incomplete, and the mistake is positive: stark or subtle color contrasts appear that will make you marvel.

RINSE
Abundant and easy.

RESULT
The leaves—their colors and transparent qualities—are magical.

USE
Integrate the leaves into other compositions. Use them as preliminary material in order to invent unique clothes, jewelry, and hats.

FEEL
From the wonder of its pure, natural state to its permanence, this paper is meant to observe and caress in your worst moments of distress. It perks us up in all types of circumstances.

Note: Chestnut trees are often plagued with diseases that manifest themselves with small points, like buttons or holes. Don't disparage these faults, they can become unique qualities when the leaves are cooked.

White Oak Paper

LOCATION
Found in woodlands and gardens in the countryside.

HARVEST
In fact, all oak trees with deciduous leaves can be used. In the summer season, cut the leaves, not the branches.

PREPARATION
Put the leaves in a pot and pour in 32 ounces (1 liter) of caustic soda per 10 quarts (10 liters) of water.

COOK
One hour and thirty minutes after it first comes to a boil. Stir often.

RINSE
Abundant and easy.

BLEACH
Pour 9 ounces (250 milliliters) of bleach in a basin of water. Mix the leaves gently. To witness the "camouflage dress" of leaves, watch the discoloration of the white oak leaves.

RINSE
Abundant and gentle.

RESULT
Not a pulp, but leaves, more solid than the leaves of a chestnut tree.

USE
The leaves are best suited to insert into your artistic compositions, though it is possible to make sheets of paper from them.

FEEL
The leaves have a precise graphic quality, so easy to identify that you can quickly become enslaved to them. Remember that you can cut, tear, and bend them as you like.

Holm Oak Paper

LOCATION
Found in woodlands, coastal regions, gardens, and along roadsides.

HARVEST
Throughout the year. Cut the leaves, not the branches.

PREPARATION
Put them in a pot and pour in 2 quarts (2 liters) of caustic soda per 10 quarts (10 liters) of water.

COOK
Four hours after it first comes to a boil. Stir often.

RINSE
Abundant and easy.

BLEACH
Pour 18 ounces (500 milliliters) of bleach in a basin of water. Mix the leaves well. Stop when you obtain the color you desire.

RINSE
Abundant and easy.

RESULT
Not a pulp, but leaves less waxy than you find in nature, and solid and thick, even becoming transparent.

USE
To integrate into your compositions.

FEEL
A feeling of having really combated nature, having broken down all the ramparts that the holm oak constructs to resist the hard life of the scrublands.

Note: After cooking, the holm oak is totally black—a very rare condition—creating truly dramatic tonalities. Take advantage of them.

Montpellier Maple Paper

LOCATION
Found in old fallow lands in the Mediterranean region.

HARVEST
In summer. Cut the leaves, not the branches.

PREPARATION
Put the leaves in a pot and pour 32 ounces (1 liter) of caustic soda per 10 quarts (10 liters) of water.

COOK
One hour after it first comes to a boil.

RINSE
Abundant and easy.

BLEACH
Pour 9 ounces (250 milliliters) of bleach in a basin of water. Mix the leaves gently. You can obtain totally transparent leaves.

RINSE
Abundant and easy.

RESULT
Not a pulp, but small leaves, very detailed in design.

USE
Leaves useful for achieving graphic details.

FEEL
Extremely light paper.

Ginkgo Biloba Paper

LOCATION
Found growing in cities and rural areas, and in parks and gardens.

HARVEST
At the end of the season. Cut the leaves, not the branches.

PREPARATION
In a pot, pour in 32 ounces (1 liter) of caustic soda per 10 quarts (10 liters) of water.

COOK
Bring the mixture to a boil. Plunge in the leaves. Stir them very delicately. Let them cook for fifteen minutes.

RINSE
Abundant and very delicate.

BLEACH
Pour 9 ounces (250 milliliters) of bleach in a basin of water. Blend the leaves gently.

RINSE
Abundant and very delicate.

RESULT
Not a pulp, but leaves of superb graphic quality.

USE
For pleasure.

FEEL
Extraordinary. You have eternalized a phoenix. The ginkgo biloba is the only tree that resisted the atomic bomb in Hiroshima.

Ginkgo and papyrus

Oleander Paper

LOCATION
Though native to northern Africa, the eastern Mediterranean, and southeast Asia, the oleander tree can be found in parks and gardens.

HARVEST
Throughout the year. Cut the leaves, not the branches.

PREPARATION
Put the leaves in a pot and pour in 32 ounces (1 liter) of caustic soda per 10 quarts (10 liters) of water.

COOK
One hour after it first comes to a boil. Stir often.

RINSE
Abundant and easy.

BLEACH
Pour 9 ounces (250 milliliters) of bleach in a basin of water. Mix the leaves well. They will become nearly transparent.

RINSE
Abundant and easy.

RESULT
Fine, long, simple leaves.

USE
Perfect for working into other paper pulp, or for pure pleasure. An oleander leaf may serve as a bookmark, to caress while reading.

FEEL
This paper has sharp edges, but is very soft.

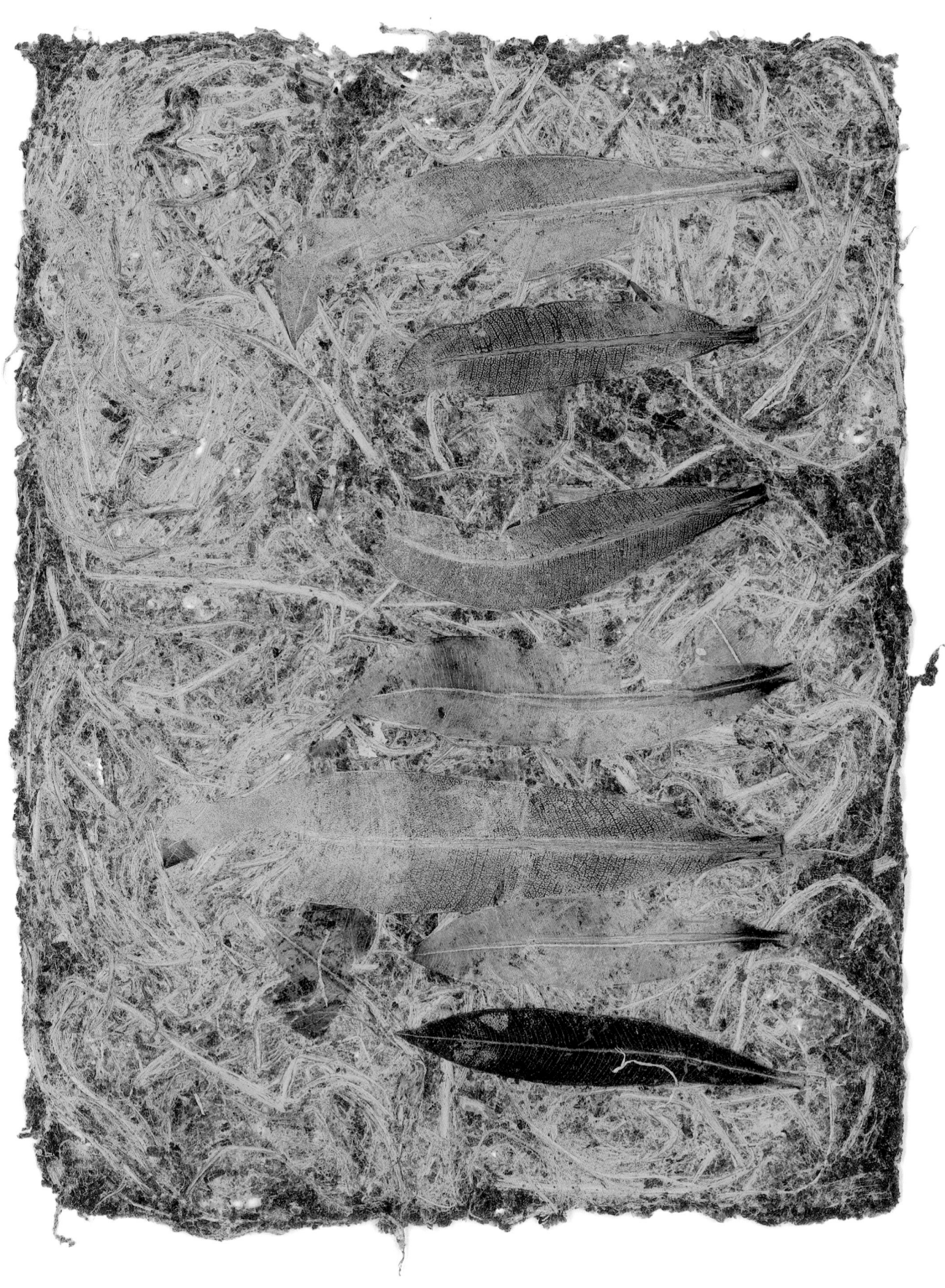

Elm Paper

LOCATION
Found in woodlands, parks, and gardens.

HARVEST
In the summer season. Cut the leaves, not the branches.

PREPARATION
Put the leaves in a pot and pour in 32 ounces (1 liter) of caustic soda per 10 quarts (10 liters) of water.

COOK
One hour and fifteen minutes after it first comes to a boil. Stir often and delicately.

RINSE
Abundant, easy, and meticulous.

BLEACH
Pour 9 ounces (250 milliliters) of bleach in a basin of water. Mix the leaves very gently. They will become completely transparent.

RINSE
Abundant, easy, and meticulous.

RESULT
A fine, delicate detail of an elm tree.

USE
Leaves that express all the sensitivities of the world, without saying a word.

FEEL
An enchantment.

Blackberry Bush Paper

LOCATION
Abundant throughout the countryside, along roadsides, and in hedgerows and gardens.

HARVEST
In the summer. Cut the leaves, not the branches.

PREPARATION
Put the leaves in a pot and pour in 32 ounces (1 liter) of caustic soda per 10 quarts (10 liters) of water.

COOK
One hour and thirty minutes after it first comes to a boil. Stir often.

RINSE
Abundant and easy.

BLEACH
Pour 9 ounces (250 milliliters) of bleach in a basin of water. Mix the pulp well.

RINSE
Abundant and easy.

RESULT
The pulp is a bit thick, with very delicate green and beige tones.

USE
For writing paper. Along with bamboo, blackberry bush pulp was used to make the first version of paper.

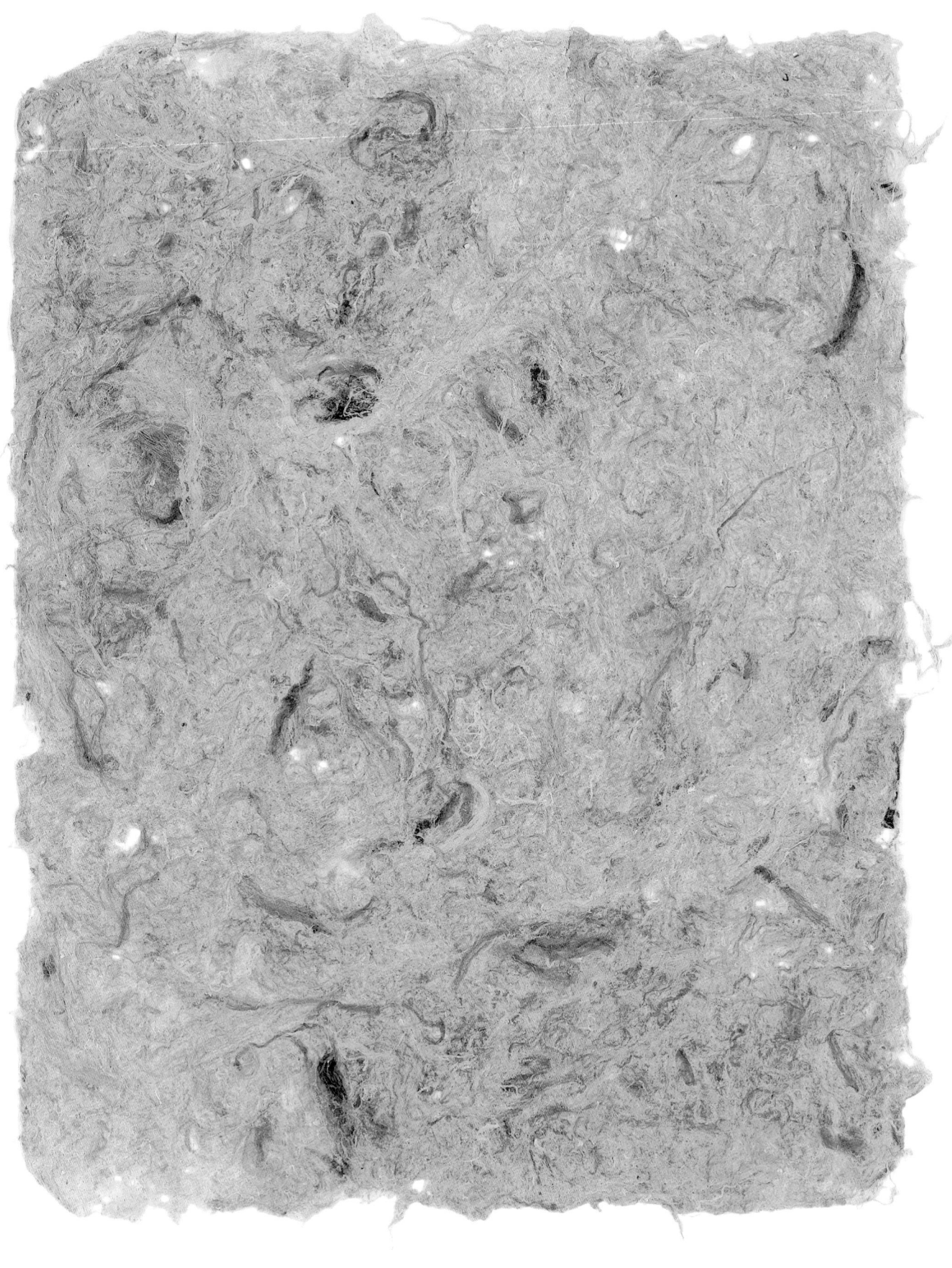

Wild Olive Paper

LOCATION
Native to the Mediterranean region, wild olive can be found in parks and gardens.

HARVEST
All year long. Cut the leaves, not the branches, because they carry the fruit.

PREPARATION
Put the leaves in a pot and pour in 32 ounces (1 liter) of caustic soda per 10 quarts (10 liters) of water.

COOK
Thirty minutes after it first comes to a boil. Stir often to keep the leaves from floating.

RINSE
Abundant and gentle.

BLEACH
Pour 9 ounces (250 milliliters) of bleach in a basin of water. Mix the leaves well. It is possible to achieve a very soft yellow color.

RINSE
Abundant and easy.

RESULT
Small leaves that have lost their waxy appearance but retained their simple form.

USE
These are very intricate sheets of paper. The olive tree is so visually complex and alive that it is impossible to add anything more on top of the paper or in the paper pulp.

FEEL
The tree of peace, a symbol of power, has such an eloquent visual quality that the addition of any further fiber, whether from a tree or plant, is unnecessary.

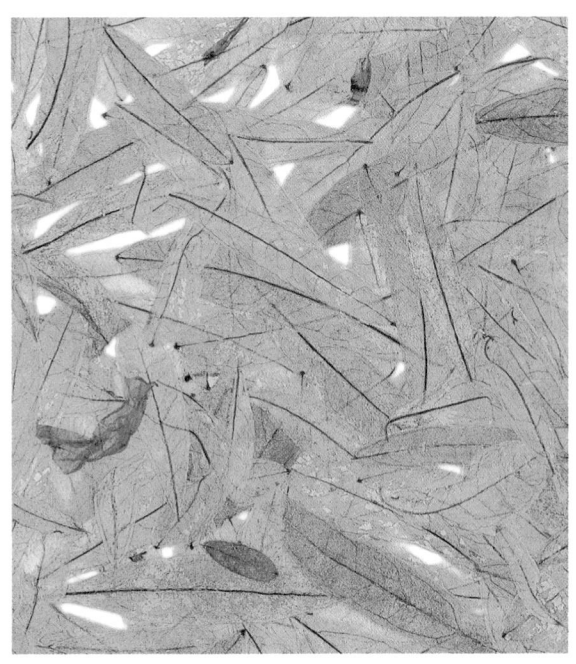

Palm Paper

LOCATION
Found growing in warm climates, and cultivated in parks and gardens.

HARVEST
Ask the maintenance services of parks and gardens. They "clean" the trees annually by plucking off the old leaves. Note: The stems can have enormous thorns.

PREPARATION
Cut the leaves in two. Put them in a pot and pour in 32 ounces (1 liter) of caustic soda per 10 quarts (10 liters) of water.

COOK
Two hours after it first comes to a boil. Stir often.

RINSE
Abundant and easy.

BLEACH
Pour 9 ounces (250 milliliters) of bleach in a basin of water. Mix the pulp well.

RINSE
Abundant and easy.

RESULT
A very fine yet fibrous pulp; very soft.

USE
A paper for writing, painting, or for pleasing.

FEEL
Soft, light, easy. An imagined vision of life.

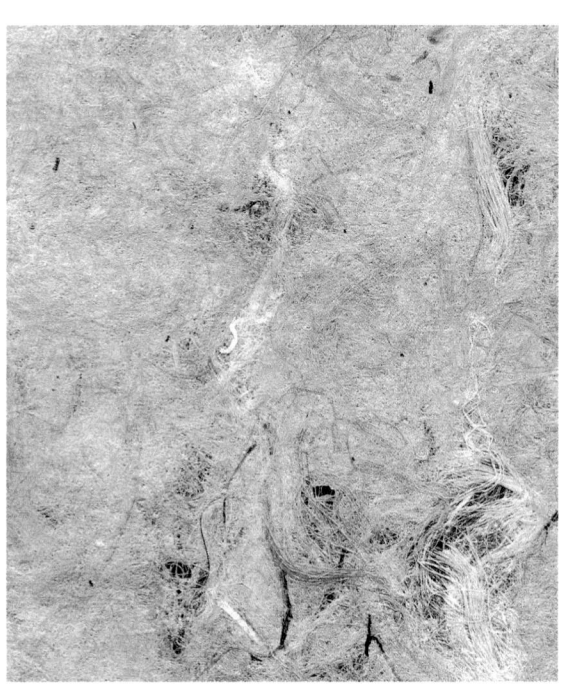

Palm and yucca

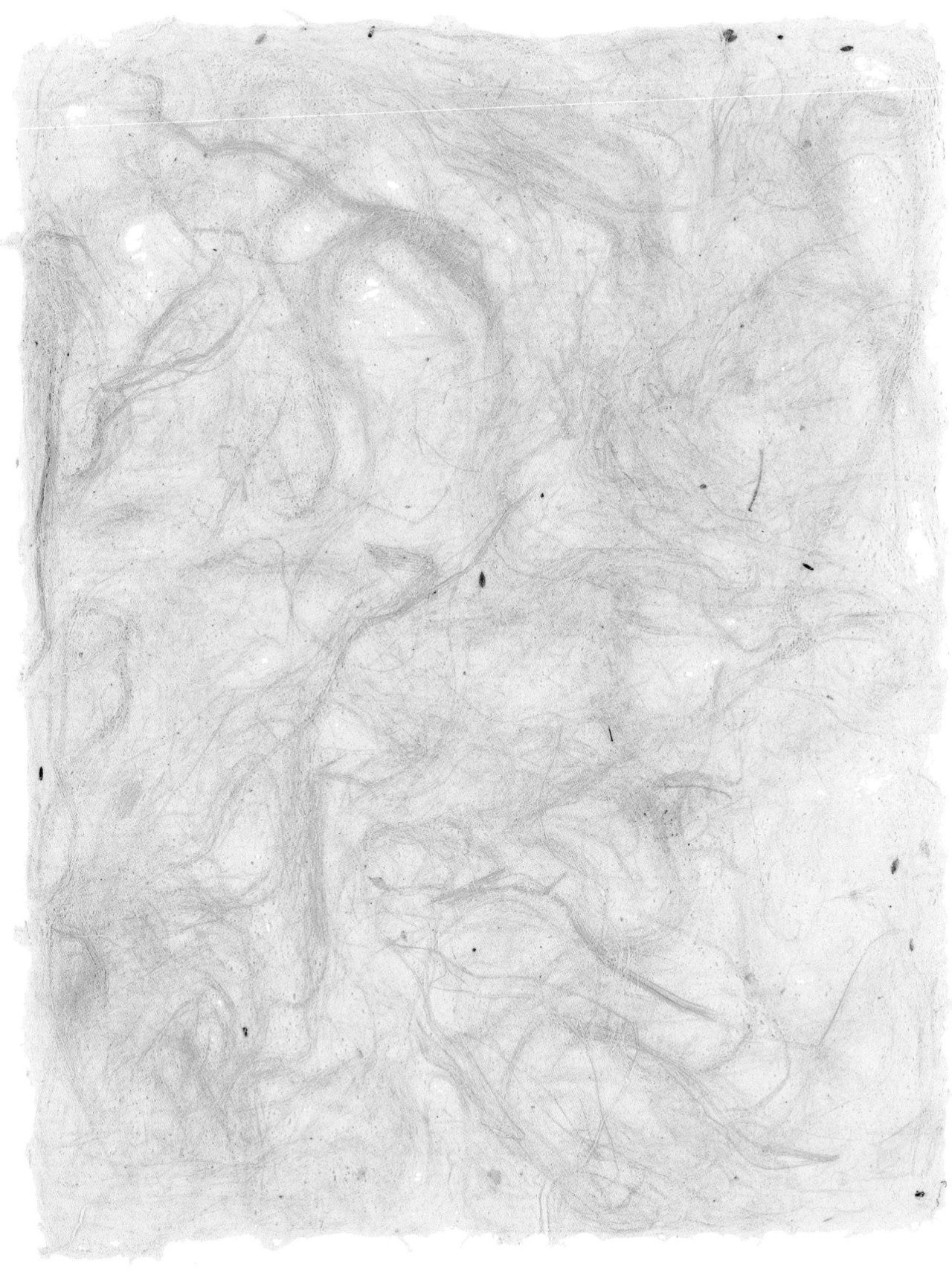

Poplar Paper

LOCATION
Widespread. Found along roads and in parks and gardens.

HARVEST
Throughout the summer season. Cut the leaves, not the branches.

PREPARATION
In a pot, pour in 32 ounces (1 liter) of caustic soda per 10 quarts (10 liters) of water.

COOK
Bring the mixture to a boil and immerse the leaves. Let them cook for approximately thirty minutes. Stir very delicately.

RINSE
Thick, delicate, and very fragile. Be sure the pressure of the water doesn't tear the leaves.

BLEACH
Pour 9 ounces (250 milliliters) of bleach in a basin of water. Mix the leaves very meticulously. You can achieve total transparency.

RINSE
Abundant, delicate, and again, more fragile than before.

RESULT
Not a pulp, but leaves. One of the most beautiful laces, fine, light, and simple.

USE
To please the eyes, for all occasions.

FEEL
The impression of having succeeded in an extraordinary magical journey. Difficult and delicate, but the pleasure is worth the price.

Pine Paper

LOCATION
Widespread. Found in parks and gardens.

HARVEST
Throughout the year. Select a variety of supple pine needles. Cut off the needles, not the branches.

PREPARATION
Put the needles in a pot and pour in 2 quarts (2 liters) of caustic soda per 10 quarts (10 liters) of water.

COOK
Three hours after it first comes to a boil. Stir often; the needles are heavy and will quickly accumulate in the bottom of the pot.

RINSE
Abundant and easy.

BLEACH
Pour 18 ounces (500 milliliters) of bleach in a basin of water. Mix the needles well. The discoloration is strange, lightening unevenly to give a speckled look. To achieve nearly white needles, repeat the bleaching process. Be patient.

RINSE
Abundant and easy.

RESULT
Not a pulp, but needles, as in nature, of another color and eternal, or nearly.

USE
The black needles can easily be used in place of a pencil to make drawings full of character. Create black lace—funereal, speckled, savage—or white, virginal.

FEEL
To have taken up a challenge: to make a fine and soft creation from sharp, pointy needles.

Note: You can use straighter, harder varieties of needles. Increase the amount of caustic soda and let them cook an hour or two more. The bleaching process is also longer.

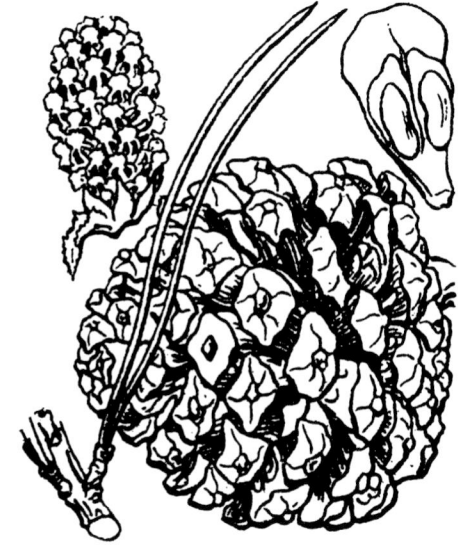

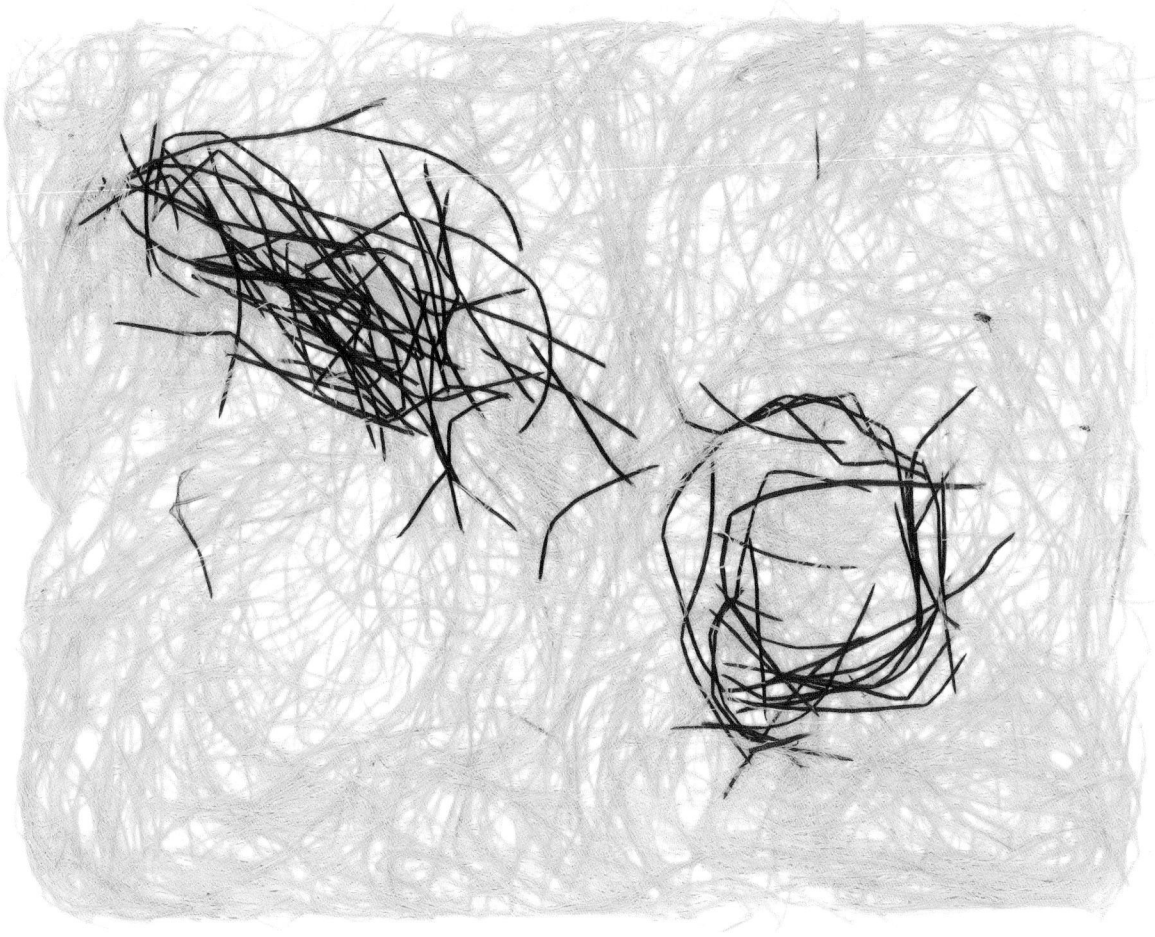

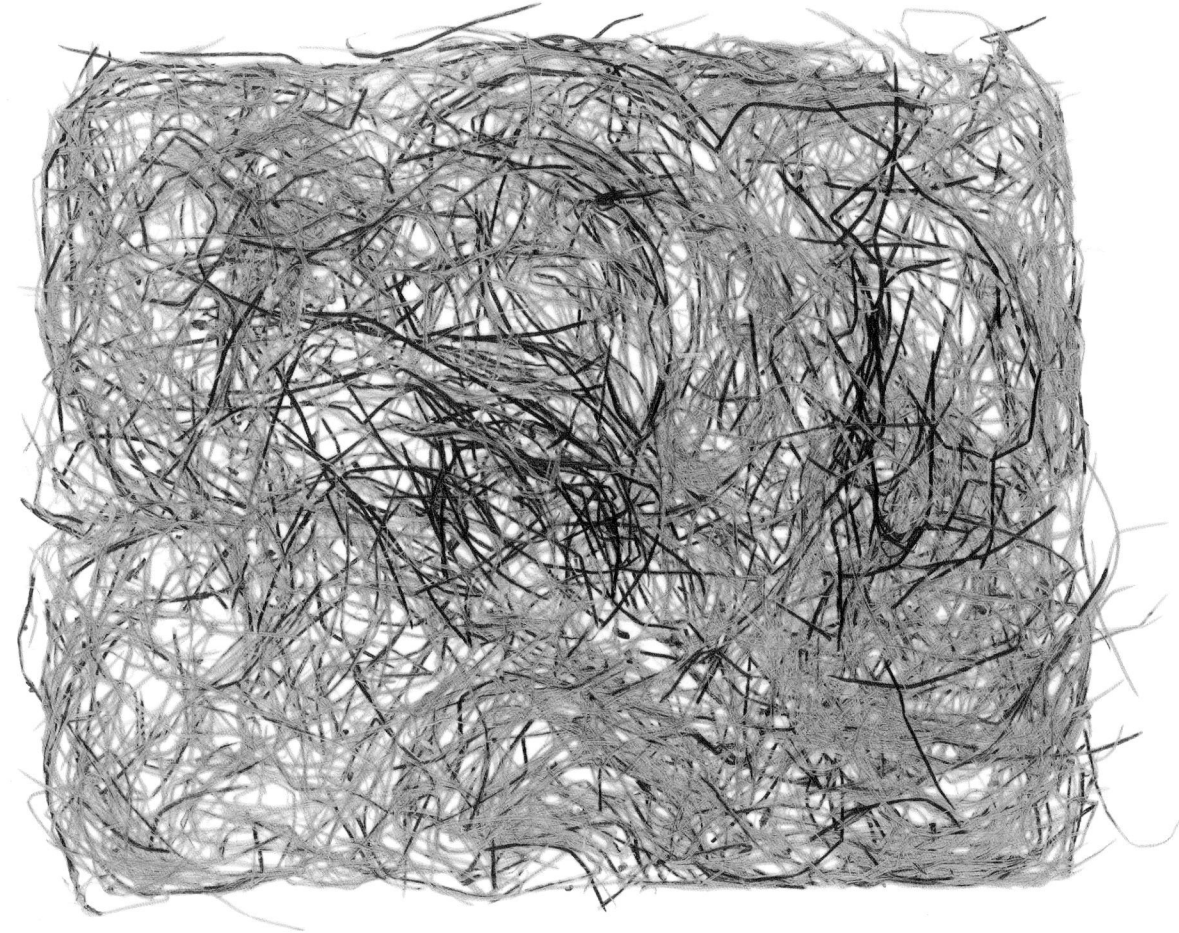

Pistachio Paper

LOCATION
Native to the Middle East, the pistachio tree can be cultivated in gardens and greenhouses.

HARVEST
In the summer. Cut the leaves, not the branches.

PREPARATION
Put the leaves in a pot and pour in 32 ounces (1 liter) of caustic soda per 10 quarts (10 liters) of water.

COOK
One hour and thirty minutes after it first comes to a boil. Stir very often; the leaves are light and float for a long time.

RINSE
Abundant and easy.

BLEACH
Pour 9 ounces (250 milliliters) of bleach in a basin of water. Stir the leaves gently. You can obtain very beautiful golds and clear yellows, so watch the discoloration process closely.

RINSE
Abundant and easy.

RESULT
Warm-colored, fragile leaves.

USE
Paper to please the eyes.

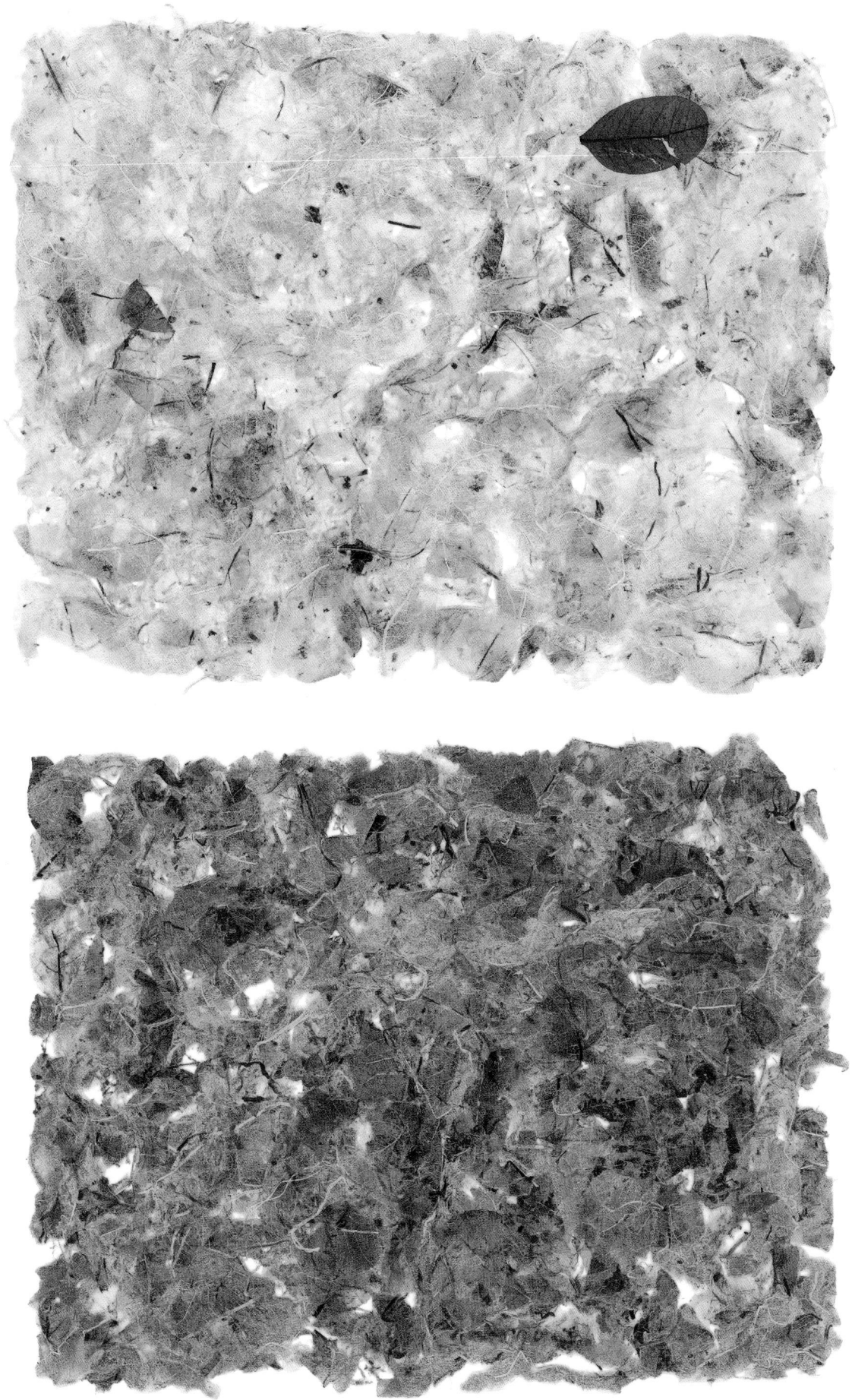

Lime Paper

LOCATION
Grown in gardens in the summer and cultivated in greenhouses.

HARVEST
In the summer, cut the leaves, not the branches.

PREPARATION
Put the leaves in a pot and pour in 32 ounces (1 liter) of caustic soda per 10 quarts (10 liters) of water.

COOK
One hour and thirty minutes after it first comes to a boil. Stir often.

RINSE
Abundant and easy.

BLEACH
Pour 9 ounces (250 milliliters) of bleach in a basin of water. Mix the pulp well. You can achieve very beautiful reds or greens, depending on the season.

RINSE
Abundant and easy.

RESULT
A pulp of fragile leaves.

USE
A perfect pulp for molding sculptures.

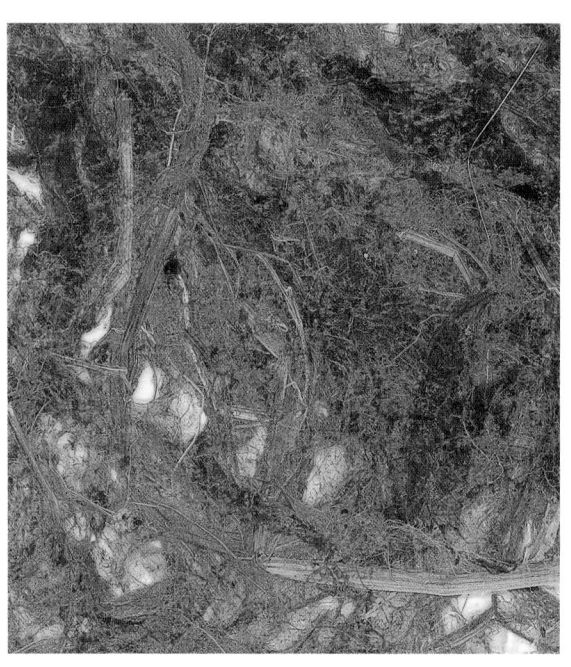

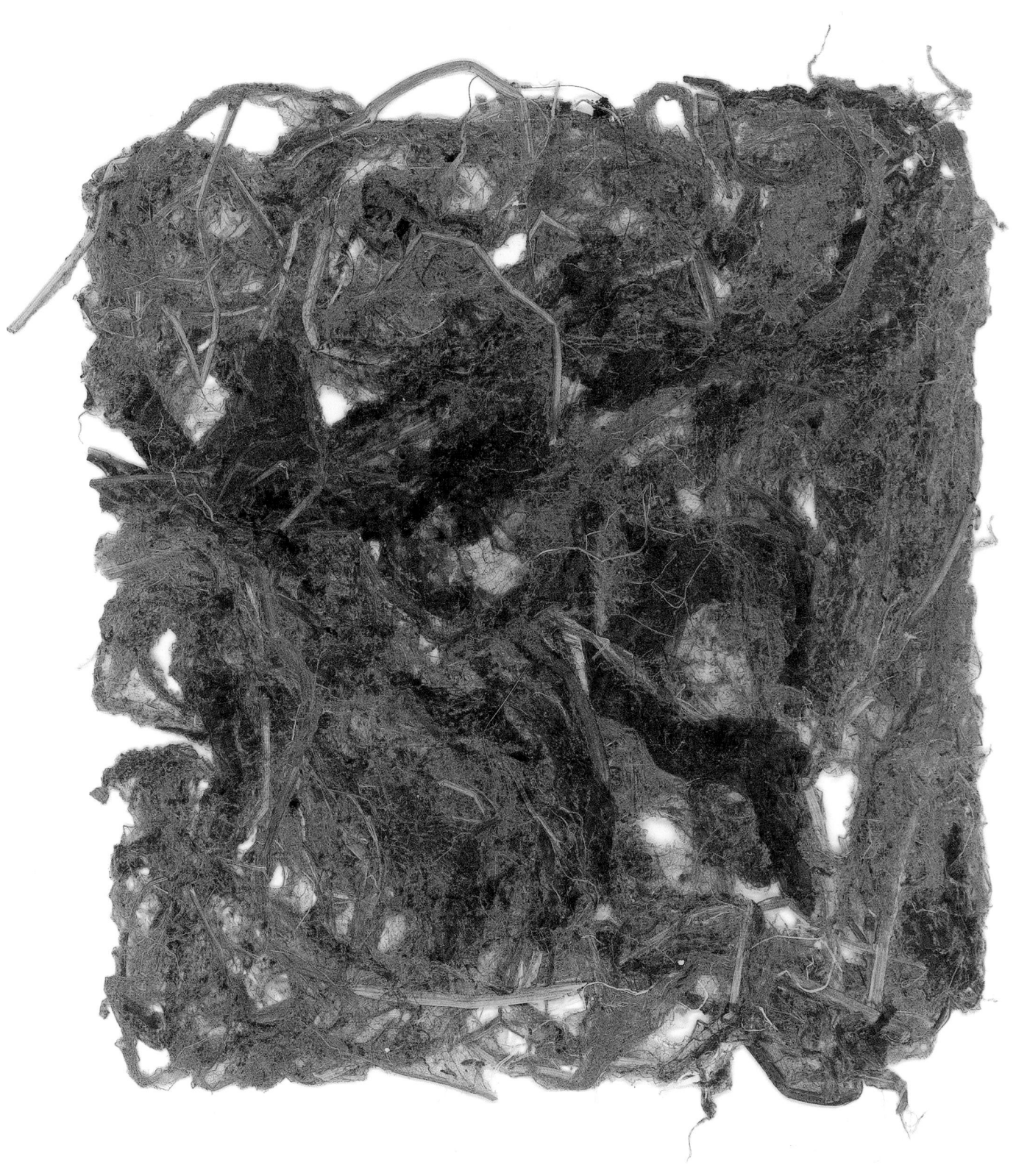

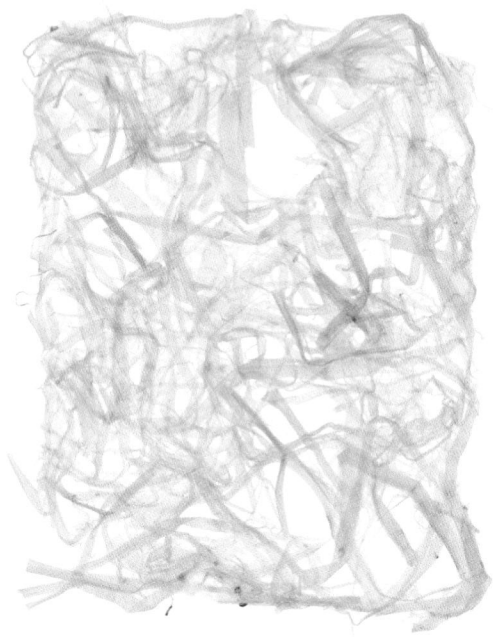

Edible Plants

Garlic skin
Artichoke
Asparagus
Eggplant (Aubergine)
Mushroom
Cranberry bean (Haricot)
Zucchini (Courgette)
Shallot skin
Wild fennel
Green bean
Bay leaf
Onion
Leek
Pumpkin
Rice
Tomato

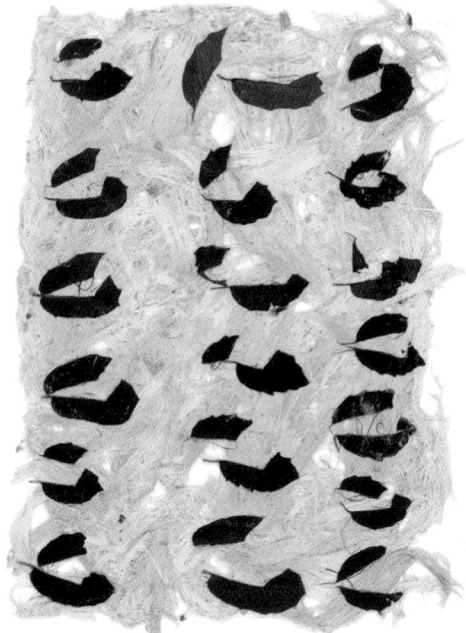

Garlic Skin Paper

LOCATION
In vegetable gardens or at the market.

PREPARATION
In a pot, pour in 32 ounces (1 liter) of caustic soda per 10 quarts (10 liters) of water.

COOK
Bring the mixture to a boil. Immerse the garlic skins. Cook them for thirty minutes, no longer. Stir well. While they cook, the garlic skins become orange, like the skins of raw shallots.

RINSE
Be very meticulous and surprisingly, the skins become white again.

BLEACH
Not necessary, since the skins are already white.

RESULT
The pulp is not very compact, and not very pleasant to touch.

USE
Paper for writing or drawing a picture.

FEEL
Like a challenge, a silly bet. A very beautiful paper on which to say things—perhaps not so very nice things. The ideal paper on which to announce a break-up.

Note: Cooking the garlic a little less will allow you to preserve the ribbon-like quality of the skins, but they will be more crumbly. You can also make paper with the leaves of the garlic plant. For this, follow the recipe for leeks.

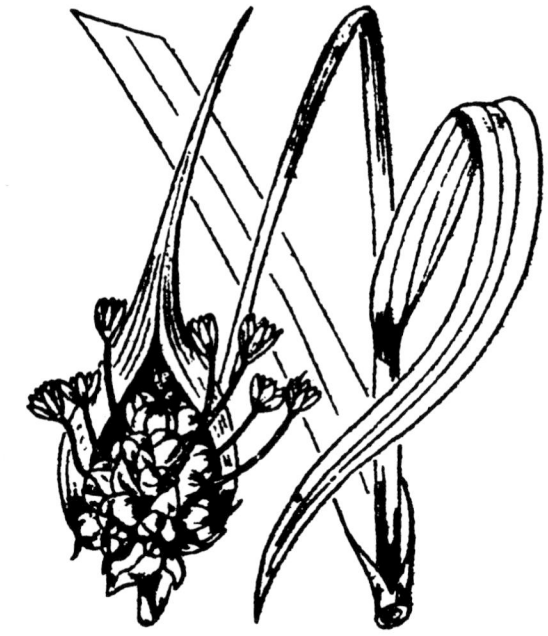

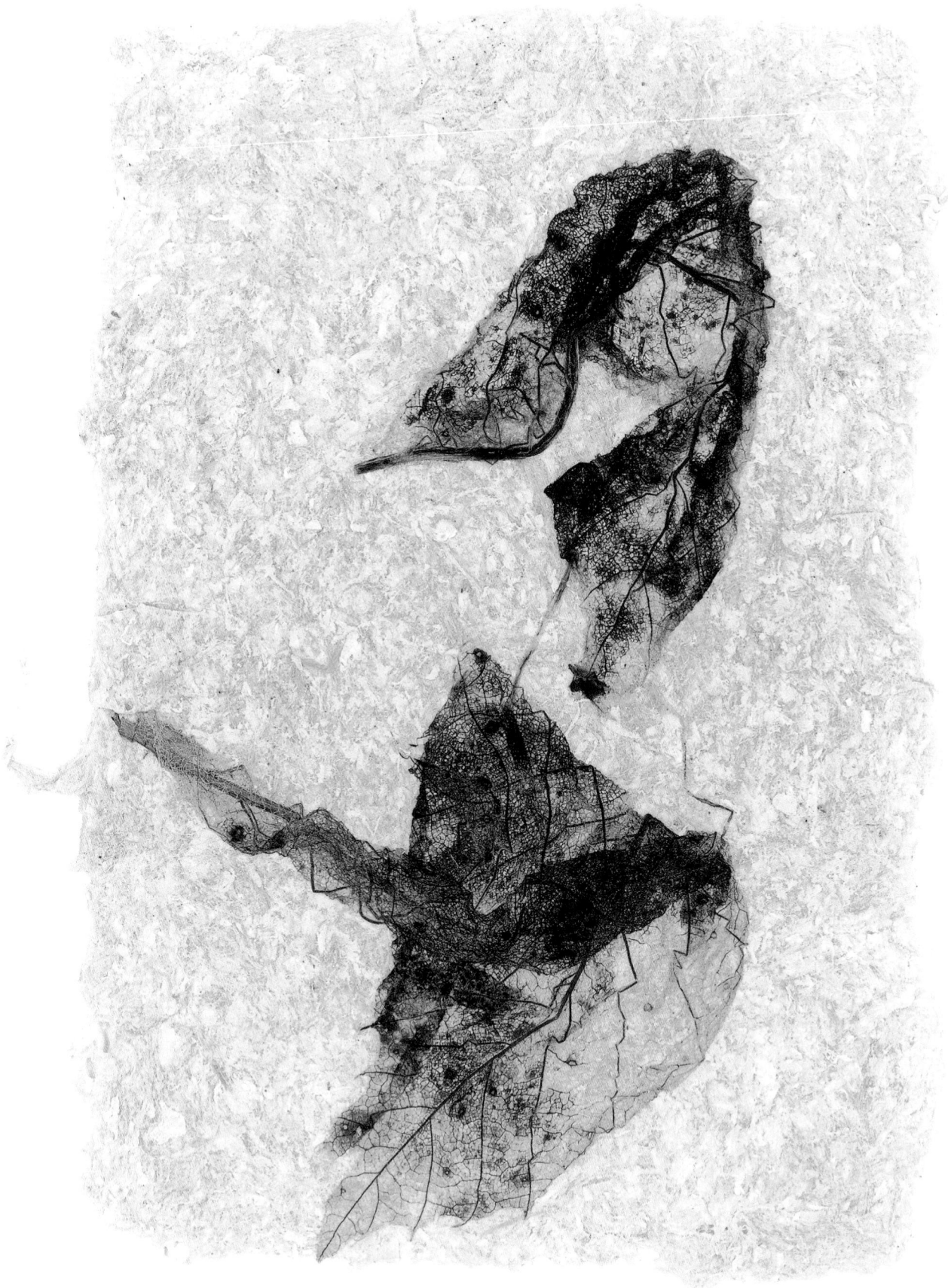

Garlic skin and chestnut

Artichoke Paper

LOCATION
In vegetable gardens and at the market.

HARVEST
More of a retrieval than a harvest. After you eat the artichoke, keep the inedible part of the leaves, or the petals. If you don't have enough after a meal, allow them to dry and wait until you have a sufficient quantity to cook them.

PREPARATION
Put them in a pot and pour in 1.5 quarts (1.5 liters) of caustic soda per 10 quarts (10 liters) of water.

COOK
Two hours after it first comes to a boil. Stir often.

RINSE
Abundant and easy. If a little "flesh" remains on the leaves, scrape it off under the water.

BLEACH
Pour 9 ounces (250 milliliters) of bleach in a basin of water. Stir the leaves well. You can obtain white fibers, but watch the discoloration because depending on the variety of artichoke, it is worth stopping. Keep the pearly colored petals. These do not age well, but the pleasure of their color can't be measured against the passage of time.

RINSE
Abundant and easy.

RESULT
Leaves with a very distinctive style. Very solid fibers, but not particularly sticky—add them as details on top of iris or leek paper.

USE
A paper made to have fun with. It's easy to make and children love to help. It's a great school activity in which to involve the parents. Collect the leaves together. It's always a great success.

FEEL
Thick, rustic.

Artichoke and holm oak

Asparagus Paper

LOCATION
In gardens and at the market.

PREPARATION
Keep the peelings from the asparagus that you eat. Allow them to dry on newspaper in a well-ventilated place until you have accumulated enough, then cook them. Place them in a pot and pour in 32 ounces (1 liter) of caustic soda per 10 quarts (10 liters) of water.

COOK
Two hours after it first comes to a boil. Stir often—dried asparagus peelings are very light and float for a long time.

RINSE
Abundant and easy.

BLEACH
Pour 9 ounces (250 milliliters) of bleach in a basin of water. Watch the discoloration of the pulp and stop it the moment the color gradations seem the most beautiful to you.

RINSE
Abundant and easy.

RESULT
The peelings keep their ribbon-like form. The sheets of paper are a bit difficult to achieve, but they are so unique when accomplished that it is worth the work.

USE
This is not a paper for writing or a paper that plays well with the light, but one that is at once rustic and pearly. Yes, that's possible.

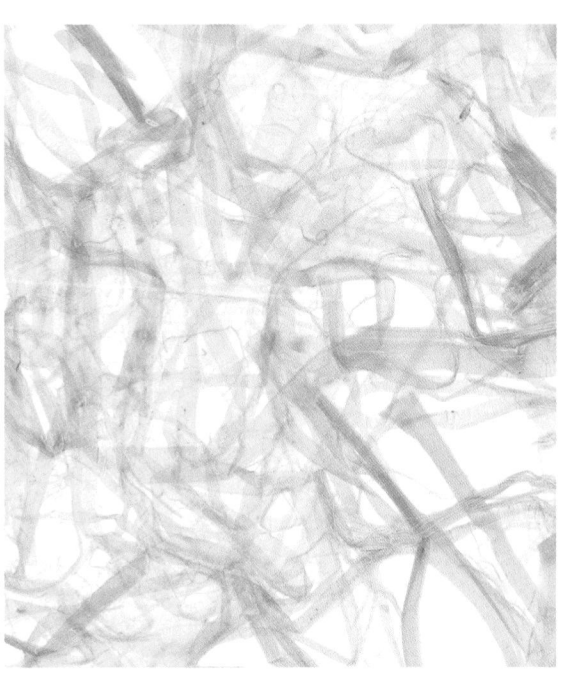

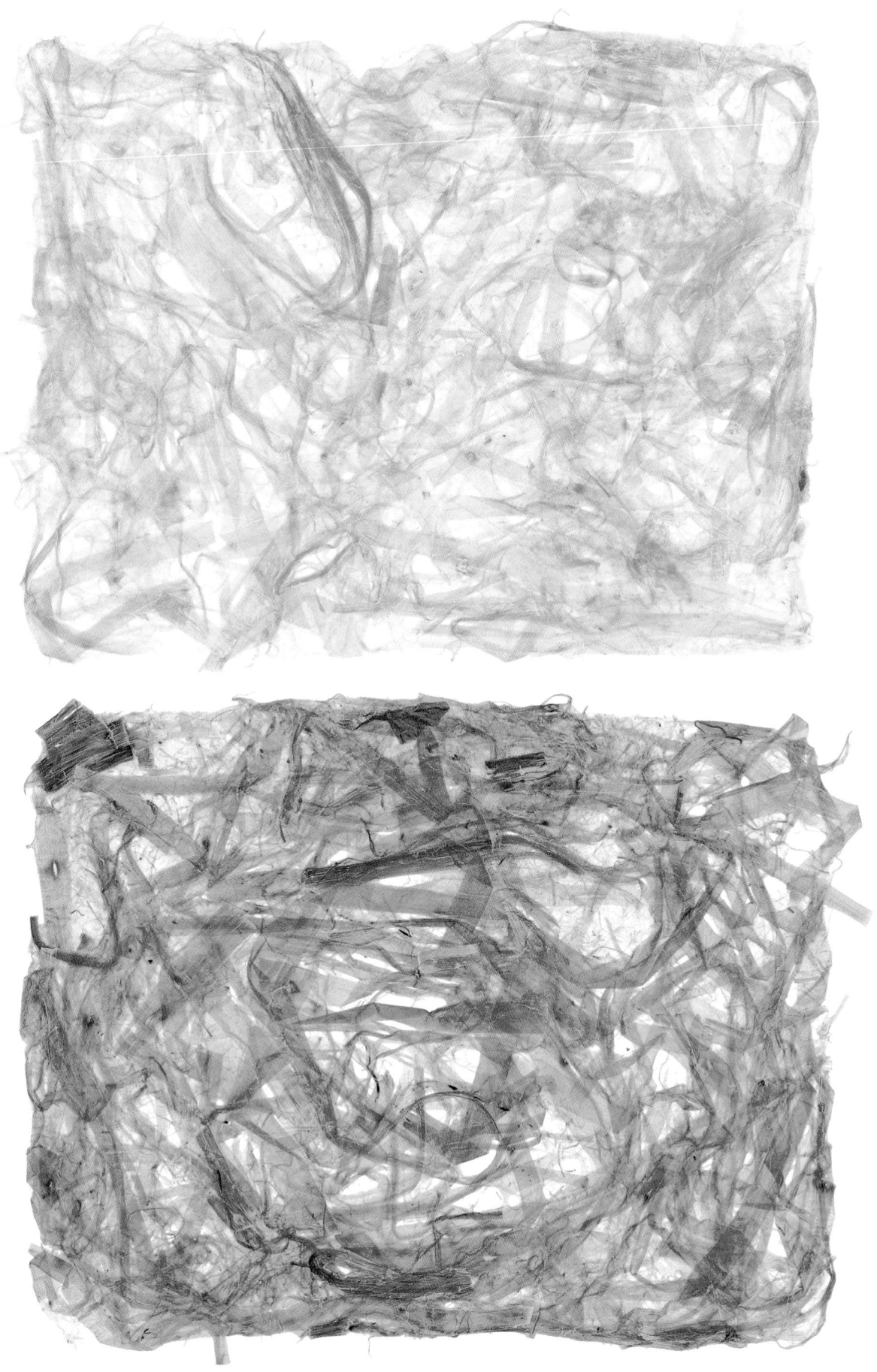

Eggplant (Aubergine) Paper

LOCATION
In vegetable gardens and at the market.

HARVEST
At the end of the season, pull out the plant from the soil. Cut off the roots and the hardest stems and throw them away. Keep the rest.

PREPARATION
Cut the plant into pieces approximately 10 inches (20 centimeters) long. Put them in a pot and pour in 32 ounces (1 liter) of caustic soda per 10 quarts (10 liters) of water.

COOK
One hour and thirty minutes after it first comes to a boil. Stir often.

RINSE
Abundant and easy.

BLEACH
Pour 9 ounces (250 milliliters) of bleach in a basin of water. Mix the pulp well. Don't go beyond a clear beige color.

RINSE
Abundant and easy.

USE
Paper for writing or painting.

FEEL
Soft.

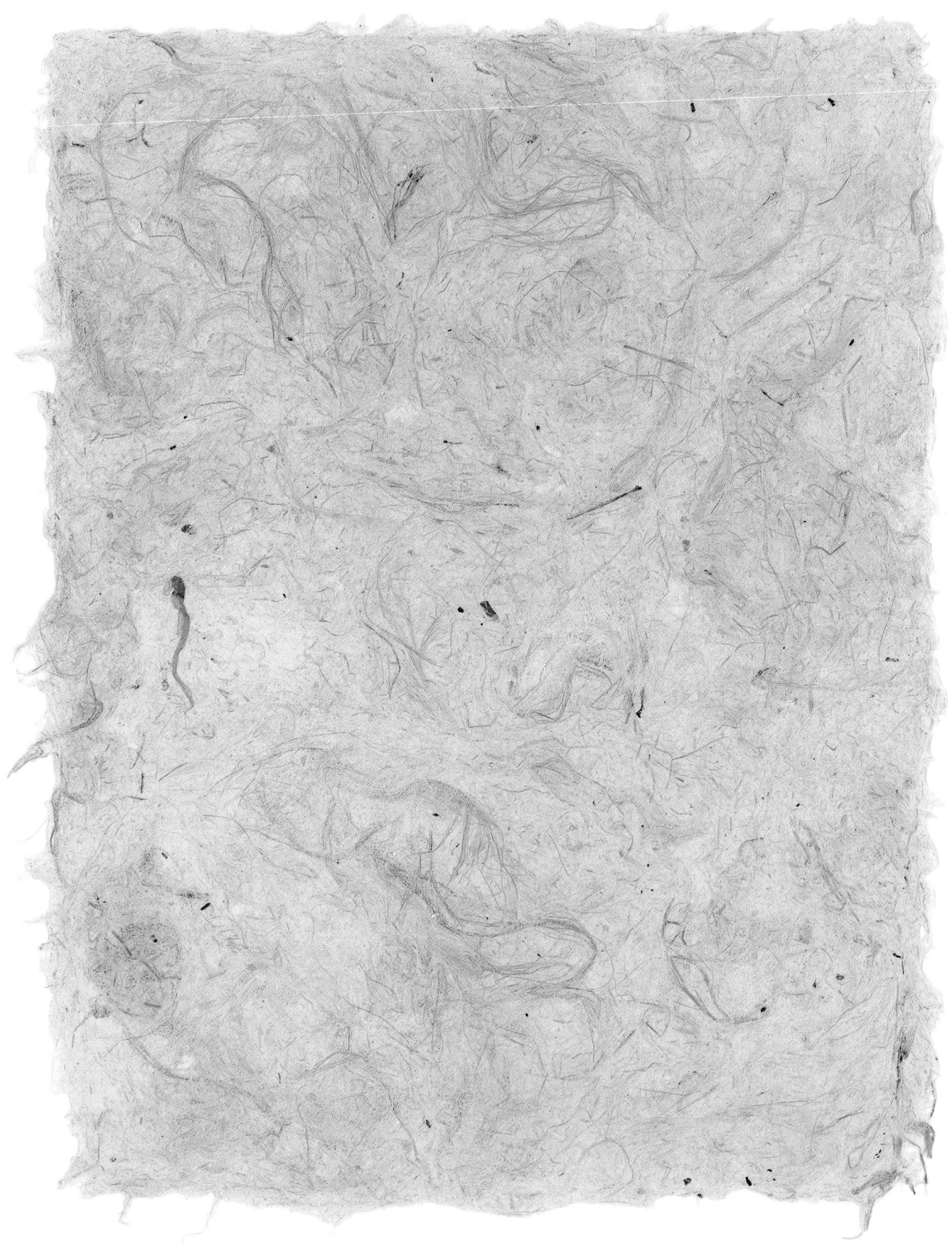

Mushroom Paper

LOCATION
In the market.

PREPARATION
Peel white button mushrooms. Keep the peels and let them dry. When you have enough, cook them.

COOK
Boil 32 ounces (1 liter) of caustic soda per 10 quarts (10 liters) of water. Immerse the mushroom peelings and cook for fifteen minutes.

RINSE
Abundant and delicate.

BLEACH
Pour 9 ounces (250 milliliters) of bleach in a basin of water. Put the mushroom pulp in the bleach mixture for only a short time.

RINSE
Abundant and very delicate.

RESULT
A very soft and fragile pulp.

USE
Reflects and plays with the light very well.

FEEL
This is a paper treasure. You need many mushrooms to produce one sheet of paper. Mushrooms are not fibrous and the paper is not very substantial, but the pleasure of having risen to the challenge is worth the work.

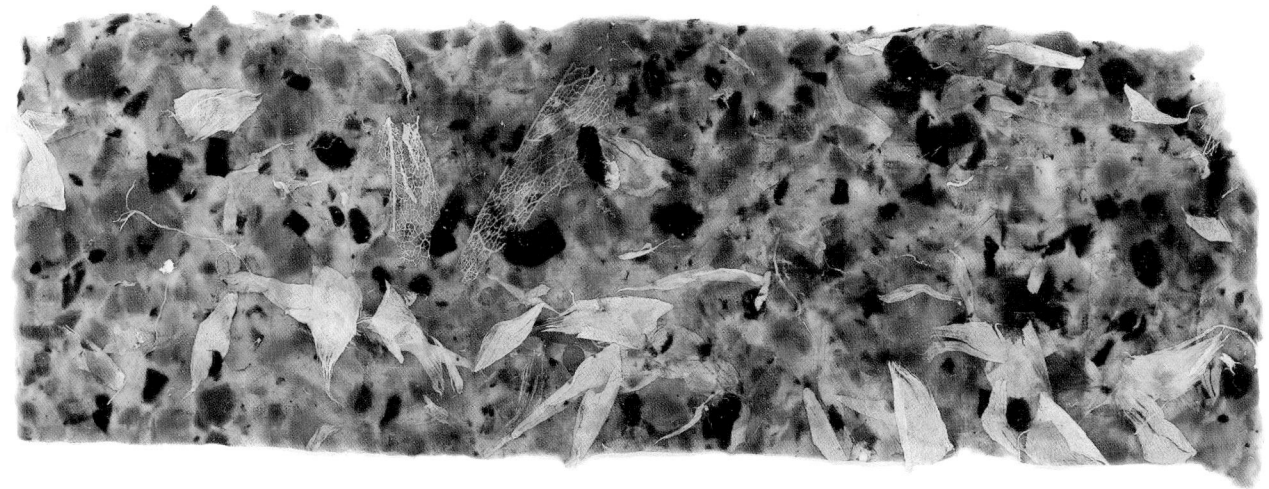

Cranberry Bean (Haricot) Paper

LOCATION
In vegetable gardens and markets.

HARVEST
In season. Each time that you eat the beans, keep the pods and dry them.

PREPARATION
Put the pods in a pot and pour in 32 ounces (1 liter) of caustic soda per 10 quarts (10 liters) of water.

COOK
Two hours after it first comes to a boil. Stir often.

RINSE
Abundant and easy.

BLEACH
Pour 9 ounces (250 milliliters) of bleach in a basin of water. Mix the pulp well.

RINSE
Abundant and easy.

RESULT
The fibers stand out according to the degree of discoloration.

USE
In compositions. For paper full of character. For pleasure.

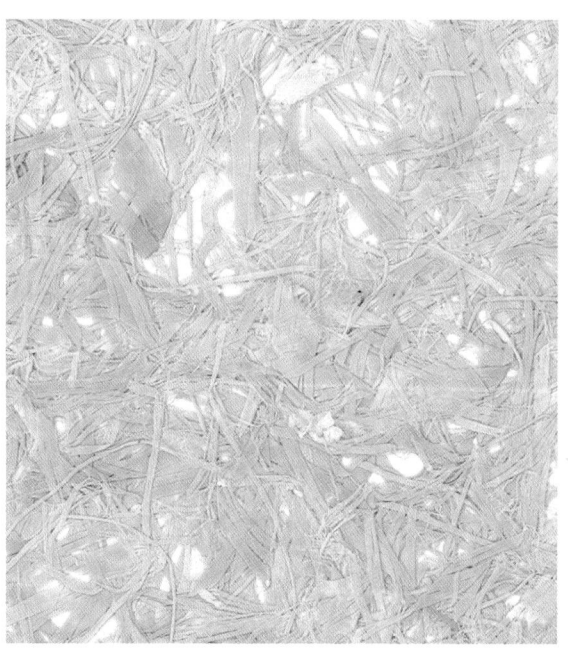

Zucchini (Courgette) Paper

LOCATION
In vegetable gardens and at the market.

HARVEST
At the end of the summer, pull up the plant.

PREPARATION
Remove the roots and the large leaves, which take up a lot of space and are not very fibrous. Cut the stems into pieces approximately 10 inches (20 centimeters) long and spread them out on newspaper to let them dry for several days. Put them in a pot and pour in 32 ounces (1 liter) of caustic soda per 10 quarts (10 liters) of water. Note that the vegetable itself can not be used, as it will fall apart if cooked in caustic soda.

COOK
One hour and thirty minutes after it first comes to a boil. Note: If the plant has not sufficiently dried, the mixture may froth too much and overflow. Stir often.

RINSE
Abundant and easy.

BLEACH
Pour 9 ounces (250 milliliters) of bleach in a basin of water. Mix the pulp well. A very soft green color is possible.

RINSE
Abundant and meticulous. The pulp becomes very fine and blocks the holes in the netting.

RESULT
A very fine pulp, easy to mold.

USE
Paper on which to write, to gently shed light.

FEEL
Smooth, fine paper for writing sweet words to devour.

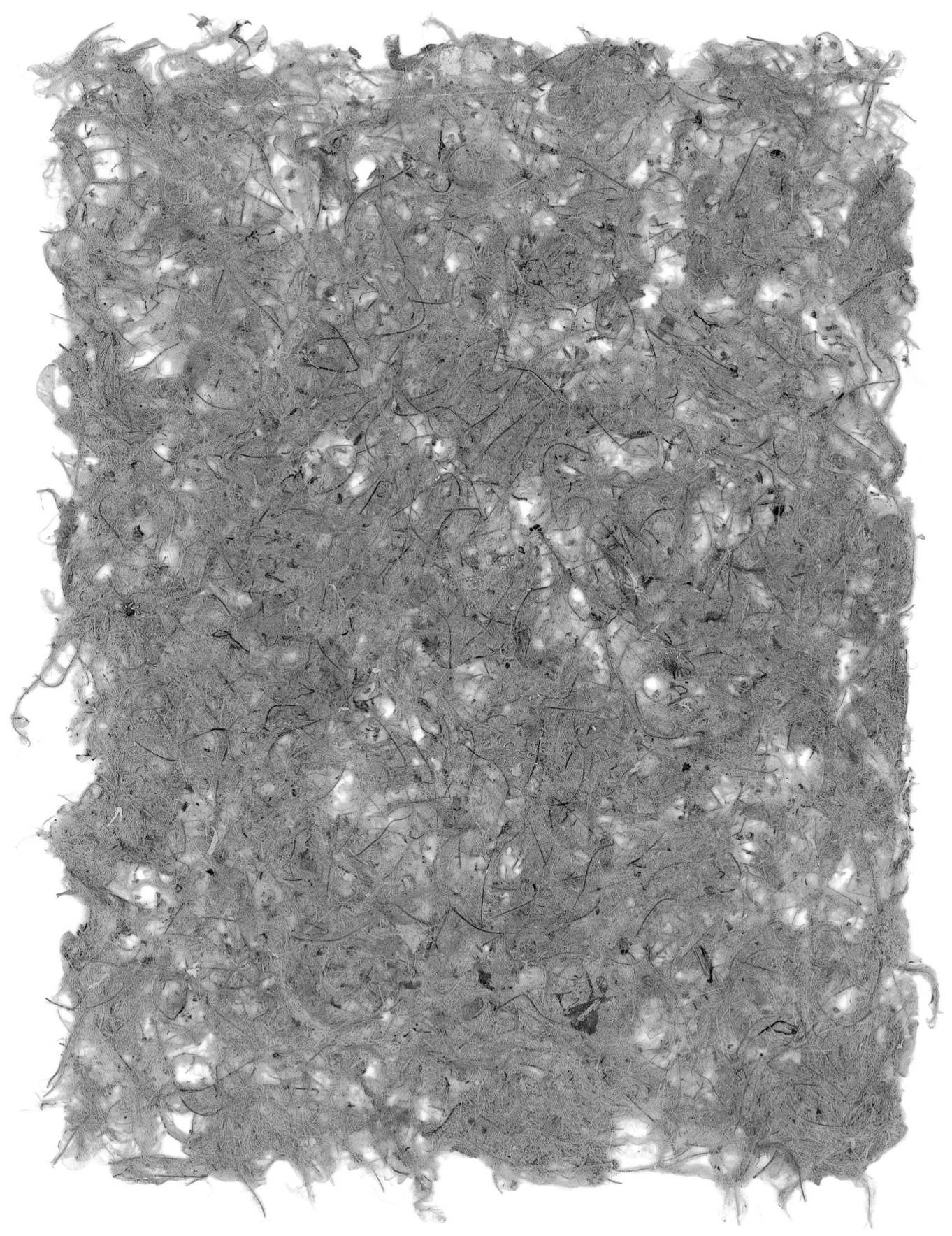

Shallot Skin Paper

LOCATION
In vegetable gardens and at the market.

PREPARATION
In a pot, pour in 32 ounces (1 liter) of caustic soda per 10 quarts (10 liters) of water.

COOK
Bring the mixture to a boil and submerge the shallot skins. Stir well because the skins are very light and float for a long time. Do not cook them longer than fifteen to twenty minutes.

RINSE
Very meticulous.

BLEACH
Pour 9 ounces (250 milliliters) of bleach in a basin of water. Watch the discoloration of the shallot skins. The process is very quick and the tonalities very subtle.

RINSE
Even more meticulous than before.

RESULT
The pulp is not very compact. During cooking, the skins are a beautiful purple color, and the bleaching process reveals a rare, delicate rose color.

USE
A material perfect for integrating into a composition. It is possible to make sheets of paper, but they are very fragile.

FEEL
Precocious, delicate—surprising for shallots, no?

Note: If you want to create paper from shallot skins, follow the recipe for onion paper.

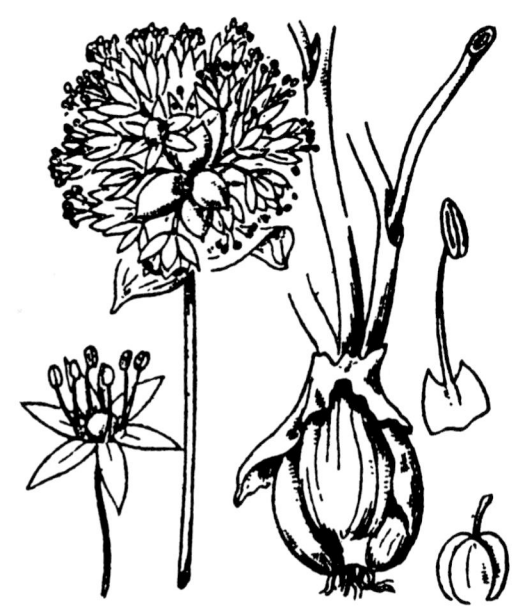

Wild Fennel Paper

LOCATION
Native to the Mediterranean region, wild fennel is cultivated in the rich soil of sunny coastal areas.

HARVEST
In the summer, when the stems begin to sprout in the woods. Pull up the stalks or cut them at ground level.

PREPARATION
Keep the leaves and the little stems. Peel the larger ones. Throw away the rest. Put everything in a pot and pour in 32 ounces (1 liter) of caustic soda per 10 quarts (10 liters) of water.

COOK
Two hours after it first comes to a boil. Stir often.

RINSE
Abundant and easy.

BLEACH
Pour 9 ounces (250 milliliters) of bleach in a basin of water. Stir the pulp well. Don't go beyond a clear beige color.

RINSE
Abundant and easy.

RESULT
The pulp is not very even or texturally homogeneous.

USE
For pleasure. This paper is not easy to write on because the fennel peelings leave ragged bits that can catch themselves on your pen. Write with a ballpoint pen, a felt-tip pen, or a pencil.

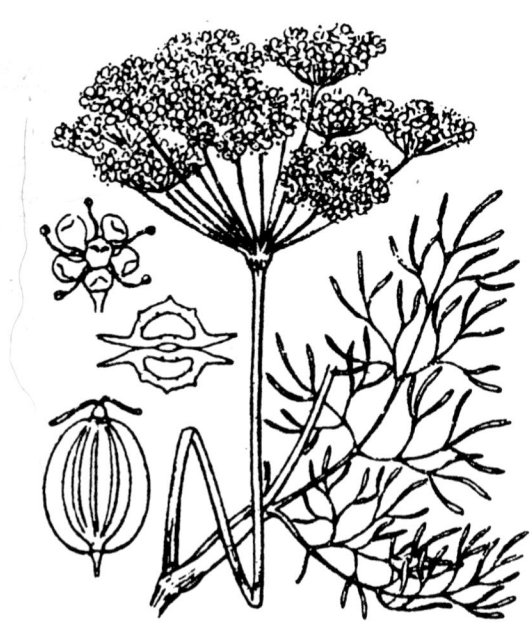

Green Bean Paper

LOCATION
In vegetable gardens.

HARVEST
At the end of harvest season, pull up the plant. Cut off the roots and the hardest stems and throw them away. Keep the rest.

PREPARATION
Cut the plant into pieces approximately 10 inches (20 centimeters) long. Put them in a pot and pour in 32 ounces (1 liter) of caustic soda per 10 quarts (10 liters) of water.

COOK
One hour and thirty minutes after it first comes to a boil. Stir often.

RINSE
Abundant and easy.

BLEACH
Pour 9 ounces (250 milliliters) of bleach in a basin of water. Stir the pulp well. Don't go beyond a clear beige color.

RINSE
Abundant and easy.

RESULT
A slightly grainy pulp, which is nevertheless homogeneous and rather fine.

USE
For writing or to use as a base: add holm oak or artichoke details, for example—plants whose pulp does not hold together very well by itself.

FEEL
The pleasure lies more in the idea than in the result. The paper is a bit rustic and smooth, but it could be said that it lacks character.

Bay Leaf Paper

LOCATION
Native to the Mediterranean, bay leaves can be found in markets.

HARVEST
Throughout the year. Cut the leaves, not the branches.

PREPARATION
Place the leaves in a pot and pour in 32 ounces (1 liter) of caustic soda per 10 quarts (10 liters) of water.

COOK
Two hours and thirty minutes after it first comes to a boil. Stir often to prevent the leaves from becoming stagnant in the bottom of the pot.

RINSE
Abundant and easy.

BLEACH
Pour 9 ounces (250 milliliters) of bleach in a basin of water. Mix the leaves well.

RINSE
Abundant and easy.

RESULT
Not a pulp, but impeccable leaves with a very simple graphic quality.

USE
The leaves are solid enough to use alone as details. It is also possible to make sheets of paper from the leaves.

Onion Paper

LOCATION
In vegetable gardens and in markets.

HARVEST
In the middle of the season.

PREPARATION
Cut the leaves off the onion plant. If you want to use the onion skins, put them aside. Place the leaves in a pot and pour in 32 ounces (1 liter) of caustic soda per 10 quarts (10 liters) of water.

COOK
Two hours after it first comes to a boil. Stir often. Throw the skins—if you are using them—in the pot fifteen minutes before the end of cooking.

RINSE
Abundant and difficult—the pulp is very solid and compact.

BLEACH
Pour 9 ounces (250 milliliters) of bleach in a basin of water. Bleach the pulp just until you achieve a clear beige color, no longer. The onion skins should remain intact and in their entirety; aim for a bronze color.

RINSE
Abundant, fragile, and difficult. The pulp blocks the holes of the netting.

RESULT
A very fine, soft pulp.

USE
The pulp and the onion skins lend themselves very well to light play. It is also possible to write on the paper.

FEEL
A smooth, rather "cold" paper that is quickly warmed by the light.

Leek Paper

LOCATION
In vegetable gardens and in markets. You can find wild leek in vineyards and along country paths.

HARVEST
In order to harvest leeks in the countryside, you must carry a small knife with you because the ground is often hard, and it would be a shame to leave the white ends. Think of making soup. Bury the small onions that encircle the head of the leek: they will allow the plant to regenerate. In vegetable gardens, it's easier.

If you buy leeks, the problem is resolved for you. The leek plant is also edible, so treat yourself to the white part. Make paper out of the green portion of the plant only.

PREPARATION
Cut the ends of the leeks into pieces approximately 10 inches (20 centimeters) long. Put them in a pot and pour in 32 ounces (1 liter) of caustic soda per 10 quarts (10 liters) of water.

COOK
One hour and thirty minutes after it first comes to a boil. Stir often; leeks stick together, particularly as they just begin to cook, and those pieces that are in the middle will not cook, or will cook poorly.

RINSE
Thick and difficult. Mix the fibers well.

BLEACH
Pour 9 ounces (250 milliliters) of bleach in a basin of water. Stir well at this step also; it's important in order to obtain a homogeneous color. You can achieve a very clear beige color, but if you remove several green fibers in the beginning of the bleaching process, you can create a lovely mixture.

RINSE
Thick and difficult; the pulp is very compact.

RESULT
The pulp is not very pleasant to touch, as it is a bit viscous. Paradoxically, while the idea of leeks itself does not immediately appeal to children, they love to touch the pulp.

USE
This can be used as writing paper, and it reflects light well. The compact pulp is ideal for adding other pieces of raw vegetable or fabric.

FEEL
A musical paper, very smooth and a bit transparent.

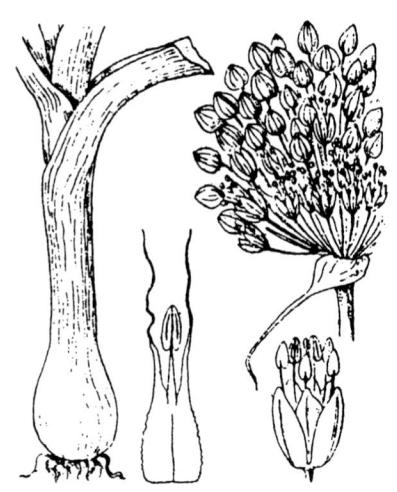

Leek and white oak

Pumpkin Paper

LOCATION
In gardens.

HARVEST
At the end of the season, uproot the plant from the ground.

PREPARATION
Cut off the roots and throw them away. Cut the stalks into pieces approximately 11 to 12 inches (28 to 30 centimeters) long. Peel the thickest parts, throwing away the rind and keeping the skin. Put everything in a pot and pour in 32 ounces (1 liter) of caustic soda per 10 quarts (10 liters) of water.

COOK
One hour and thirty minutes after it first comes to a boil. Stir often.

RINSE
Lush and easy.

BLEACH
Pour 9 ounces (250 milliliters) of bleach in a basin of water. You can obtain a very clear beige pulp.

RINSE
Thick and easy.

RESULT
The pulp is homogeneous and soft.

USE
Great for writing paper, among other uses.

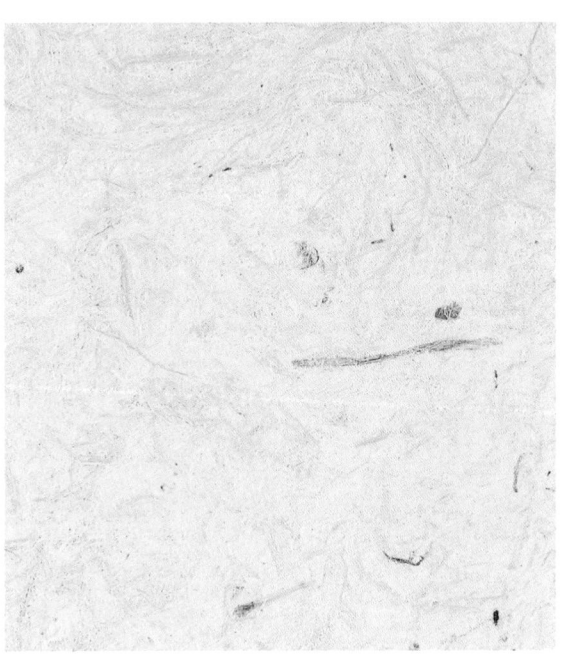

Rice Paper

LOCATION
In rice paddies.

HARVEST
At maturity. Harvest the entire plant except the roots. Remember to ask permission from the owner of the rice fields.

PREPARATION
Cut the plant in two. Put it all in a pot and pour in 32 ounces (1 liter) of caustic soda per 10 quarts (10 liters) of water.

COOK
Two hours after it first comes to a boil. Stir often.

RINSE
Heavy and easy. Pay attention: Don't lose any of the fine pulp.

BLEACH
Pour 9 ounces (250 milliliters) of bleach in a basin of water. Mix the pulp well. The ideal is to achieve a pulp that is nearly white with golden-yellow grains.

RINSE
Thick and difficult.

RESULT
The pulp becomes very, very fine.

USE
This is a superb and very interesting paper. The rice grains cause the pulp to become so thick that you can easily make sculptures from it. If you decide not to use the rice grains, the pulp is fine, smooth, and nearly common-looking; a metamorphosis.

FEEL
Soft and solid.

Note: Changing the cloths is a delicate process in this case because the starch in the rice makes the paper stick.

Tomato Paper

LOCATION
In vegetable gardens and in markets. At the end of the season, after harvest, pull up the plant.

PREPARATION
Remove the roots and throw them away. Cut off and keep the small stems and leaves. Cut the stems into pieces approximately 10 inches (20 centimeters) long. Peel the thicker stems. Put everything in a pot and pour in 32 ounces (1 liter) of caustic soda per 10 quarts (10 liters) of water.

COOK
One hour and thirty minutes after it first comes to a boil. Stir often.

RINSE
Easy and abundant.

BLEACH
Pour 9 ounces (250 milliliters) of bleach in a basin of water. Mix the pulp well. Do not stir beyond achieving a clear green or clear beige color.

RINSE
Thick and delicate. The bleaching process makes the finest fibers very fragile.

RESULT
A very fine pulp with translucent ribbons (the peelings).

USE
For writing. Paper on which to dream.

FEEL
An ambiguous sensation of being both soft and tough (the peelings).

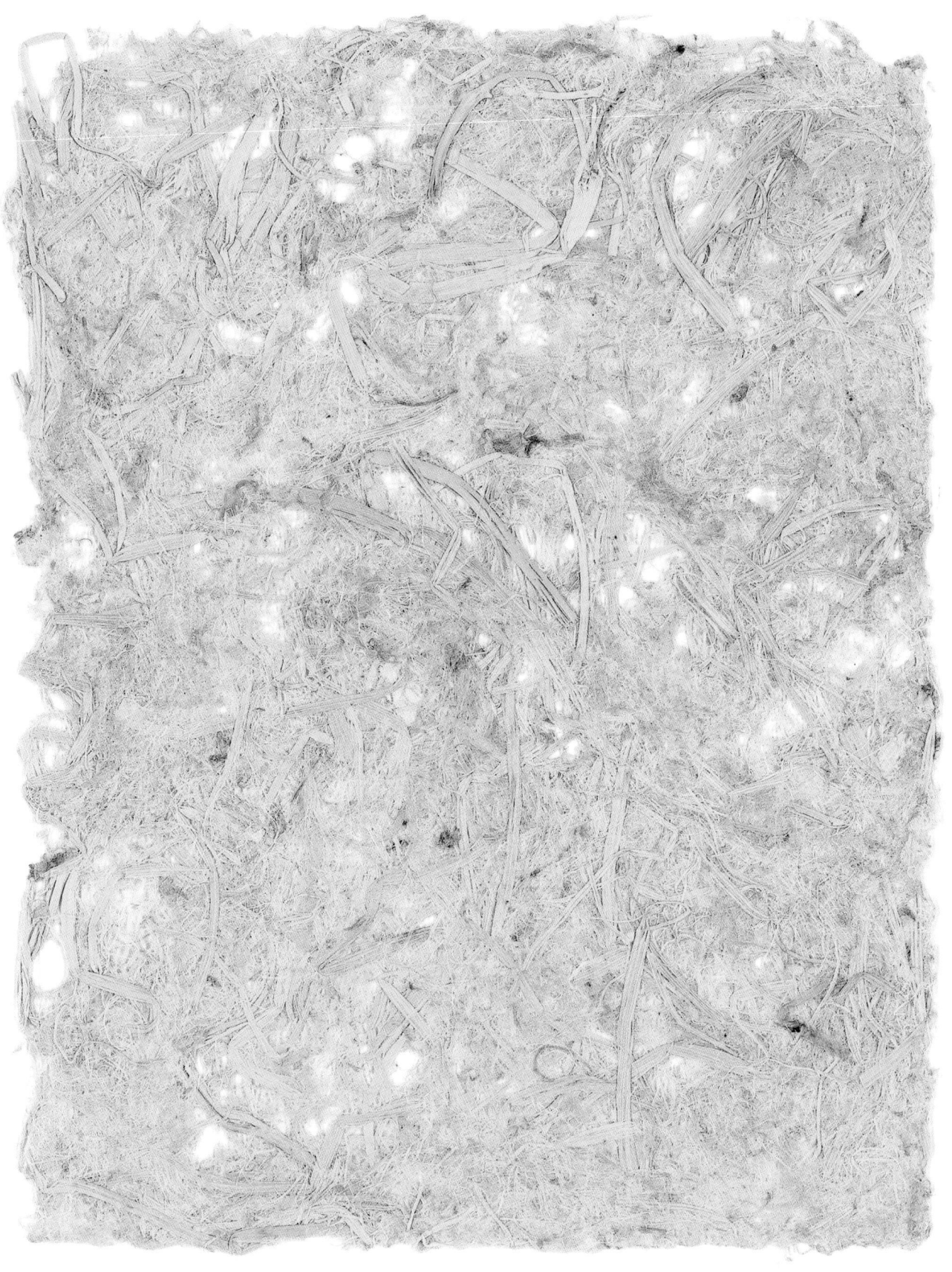

Non-plant Papers

Wasp Nest Paper

A wasp's immediate environment determines its nest. Its form depends upon its location—between a window and a shutter, in the depths of a house, or in the crook of a tree.

Its color depends upon the vegetation used to create it—beiges, browns, grays, and very subtle shades of pink.

You can use wasp or hornet nests. Be sure the nest is untenanted, or get help in disposing of the wasps. Propose an exchange: a nest of wasps for several sheets of handmade paper. This way, you will both be happy.

PREPARATION

Using a spatula, lift a sheet of paper of medium thickness from the mold and deckle—iris paper, oat paper, or another kind. Be gentle and patient. You can determine the size of the sheet yourself. If you are too rough with the mold and deckle or remove the paper too early, begin again. Papermaking is an agreeable endeavor because we always have the right to make mistakes.

Gently immerse the nest in a basin of clean water, then place it on top of the piece of paper. Cover everything with a piece of cloth, apply the press, and . . . there you have it!

Children love this, perhaps because it's easy, perhaps because they have the impression of having tamed the wasp.

In any case, they are not at the end of their discovery because behind paper walls are . . . the buildings where all these pests live. And that is beautiful, but it is another story . . .

Wasp nest and recycled paper

Wasp nest, papyrus, and ginkgo biloba

Recycled Paper

• Old paper

Avoid newsprint—the quality is poor and it is too covered in writing. It will make a sad, ugly pulp because it is saturated with ink. It is better to use scraps of writing paper, old notes that you have received, or scratch paper.

• Mixer

If you do not have one, it doesn't matter. Use your hands, mixing the pulp while a movie is playing on the television, or better yet, enlist the help of children—they will really enjoy it.

• Two basins

One for the pulp and another to make the sheets of paper.

• Sieve (mold and deckle)

Made to any dimension you wish, but be sure that it is smaller than the basin.

• Rags, sponge, press (or clamp), and two plywood boards

PREPARATION

Tear the paper into small pieces or crumple it up without crushing it. Put the paper in the basin and pour in enough water to just cover it. Let the mixture soak overnight. If you are in a hurry, use hot water. Ideally, the paper will be soaked with water after resting in the bottom of the basin. Place the paper in the mixer; the original sizing is still there, in suspension, so there is no need to add more. If you do not have a mixer, toss and retoss until the pulp becomes fine and soft. Fill the second basin with clean water. Add one or two handfuls of pulp. (It is difficult to specify the amount because it depends on the amount of water, the size of the mold and deckle, and the speed with which the sheet of paper is actually made). So, the only solution is to test and experiment with each attempt.

Mix the pulp in the water well.

Spread some of the pulp on the mold and deckle. Take both the parts of the mold and deckle in both hands. Don't forget to keep the frame with the netting (the mold) underneath the deckle; the netting itself should face up.

Lower the mold and deckle vertically into the basin until the water covers it completely. When it touches the bottom, tip it so it's level and remove it from the basin. This last step must be done in one quick motion—it only requires a turn of the wrist, as you will discover. The faster the motion, the finer your piece of paper. The

Recycled paper and chestnut leaves

150

slower the motion, the thicker your piece of paper will be—like cardboard, if you have used a lot of pulp. If the mold and deckle are not completely level while you remove them from the water, the paper will be thicker towards the lower side. Be careful.

Allow the excess water to run off. Place the mold and deckle on the side of the basin and delicately remove the mold (bottom frame). Let the water drain off a bit more if necessary. Lay a rag on the table, making sure it does not have any folds or creases in it.

Lay one side of the mold and deckle on the rag, the pulp facing away from you. Rap the screen on the rag in one quick, forceful motion. Sponge off any excess water from the netting. Delicately remove the mold and deckle.

Is the paper just as you want it? Are the sides straight? Does it have proper right angles? If yes, bravo! If not, don't hesitate to begin again to get it just right. Fold the rag over the sheet of paper and place it under the press.

Recycled paper and knitting yarn

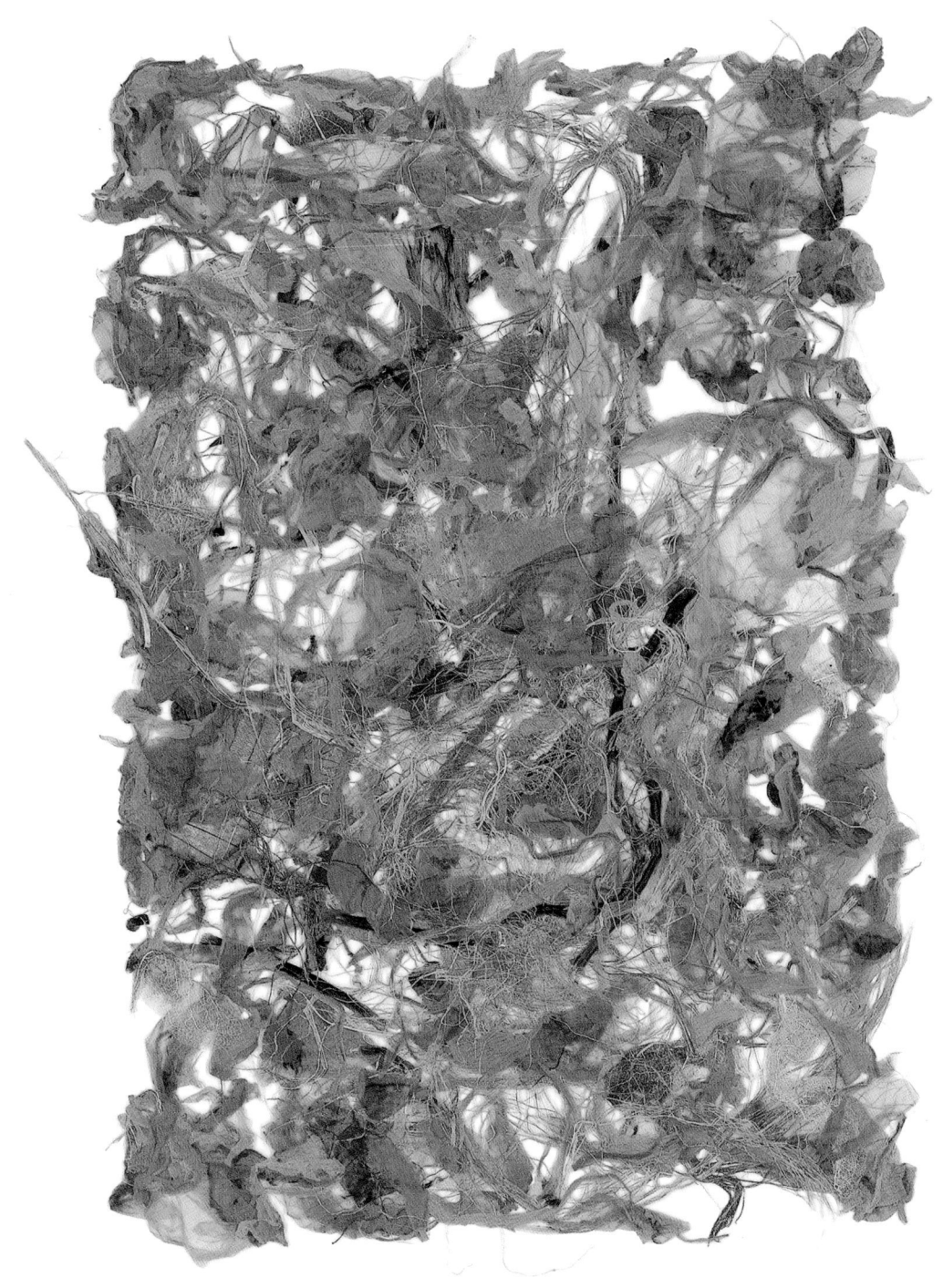

Nine Artists
of Plant Paper

The rapport between paper and artist is one of complicity and inspiring trust. There is no such thing as writing on a virgin surface. Before touching pen to paper, before dog-earing a page, before the first splash of paint, the writer, the calligrapher, the folder of paper, or the painter knows that the material already has a history.

We realize this before even choosing the material; we consider the grain, the thickness, the feel, the color, the plant itself.

In other words, the work does not begin with form but with content, which seems clichéd, but . . .

When the heart beats too quickly or, quite the contrary, shrivels up, when hairs bristle, ears buzz, nostrils quiver, eyes shine, it's because cerebral or emotional maturation has reached its peak.

The act of creation and of making paper engages our bodies. For some, it begins in a workshop, for others, in a field, for others still . . . elsewhere.

The act of creation is a bit intellectual but, in particular, very physical, concrete—the idea doesn't suffice. For this reason artists need involvement with their material.

Our idea, a small light buried in our bodies that allows itself to penetrate and infiltrate who we are, what we know we are, and what we ignore, delightfully divulges all our secrets, even the worst, to bring them out into the open.

Beautiful, ugly, small, large. Like a mirror. Be a fairy and a witch at the same time.

Poplar

Ivy

Mary-Lise BEAUSIRE
Yvonne CABANIS
Marie-Thérèse HERBIN
Marie-Claire MEIER
Ruth MORO
Aurelia MUÑOZ
Pascale PASELLO
Jean-Paul RUIZ
Hiltrud SCHÄFER

Like a bouquet of free spirits,
arranged in an arbitrary way,
subjective.

Artists choose
according to who they are,
according to what they make.

Everything begins
in the fields,
continues in the kitchen,
transforms itself
in the workshop,
reveals itself in this book,
explodes in your mind.

For you to create!

Mary-Lise Beausire

9 Rue des Champs du Bourg, 920 Martigny 2, Valais, Switzerland

Once all the necessary ingredients are compiled, I cook the plants so they break down and I sometimes dye them in preparations of my own making. The goal is to emphasize the plant fibers which become, from then on, the vocabulary of my expressions with plants—both the container and the contents of the pages that I create. As for the rest of the paper, it occurred to me to insert calligraphic marks composed of fibrous elements that evoke the texts of ancient manuscripts. This technique gives me the feeling of reestablishing, to a certain degree, the equilibrium that I destroyed by uprooting the plants from their natural environment in order to imbue them with a new life, in another form.

Mary-Lise Beausire

Mary-Lise Beausire's work engages in a body-to-body partnering with nature, imbuing it and later telling its story by way of an organic writing paper, a witness to this exceptional experience. As for us, the spectators, we are invited to share in a rapport equally tactile and visual, in this face-to-face with the work that incites contemplation, harmony, and a rejuvenation of artistic possibility. Because, surely, what we are dealing with here are books that create a sense of peace, soft lights, and writings to decode—while pricking up our ears—to listen to the rustle and the breath, not of the paper, but of the soul.

Philippe de Bellet

Mary-Lise Beausire is a member of the International Association of Hand Papermakers and Paper Artists (IAPMA), among others. Her works can be found in public collections from Tallinn (Estonia) to Barcelona (Spain). She exhibits in Switzerland, where she lives, in Italy, Great Britain, and in the United States, alone and with other artists.

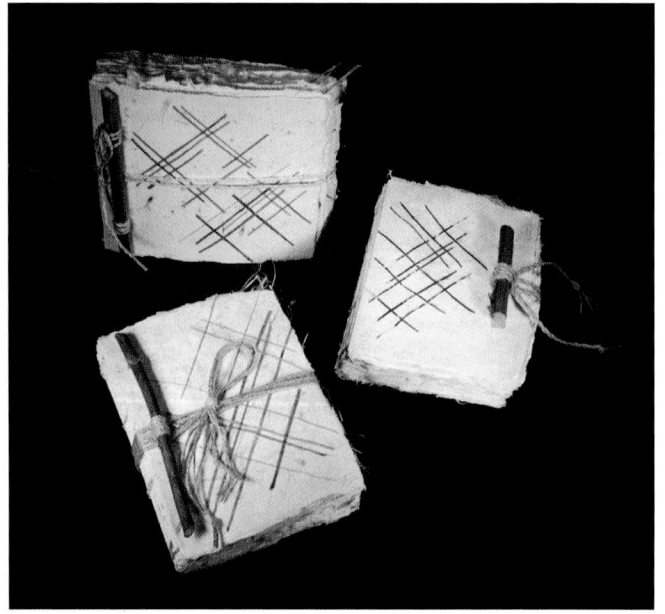

1

2

1. Spirit of nature (wheat straw), 1997
2. Meditation journals I, II, III (bamboo, bulrush, lavender), 1997
3. Roll-Unroll IV (wheat straw), 28 x 20 x 12 cm, 1997
4. Roll-Unroll V and IV (miscanthus), 22 x 16 cm, 1997

Photographs: Jacqueline Bertelle (1920 Martigny, Switzerland)

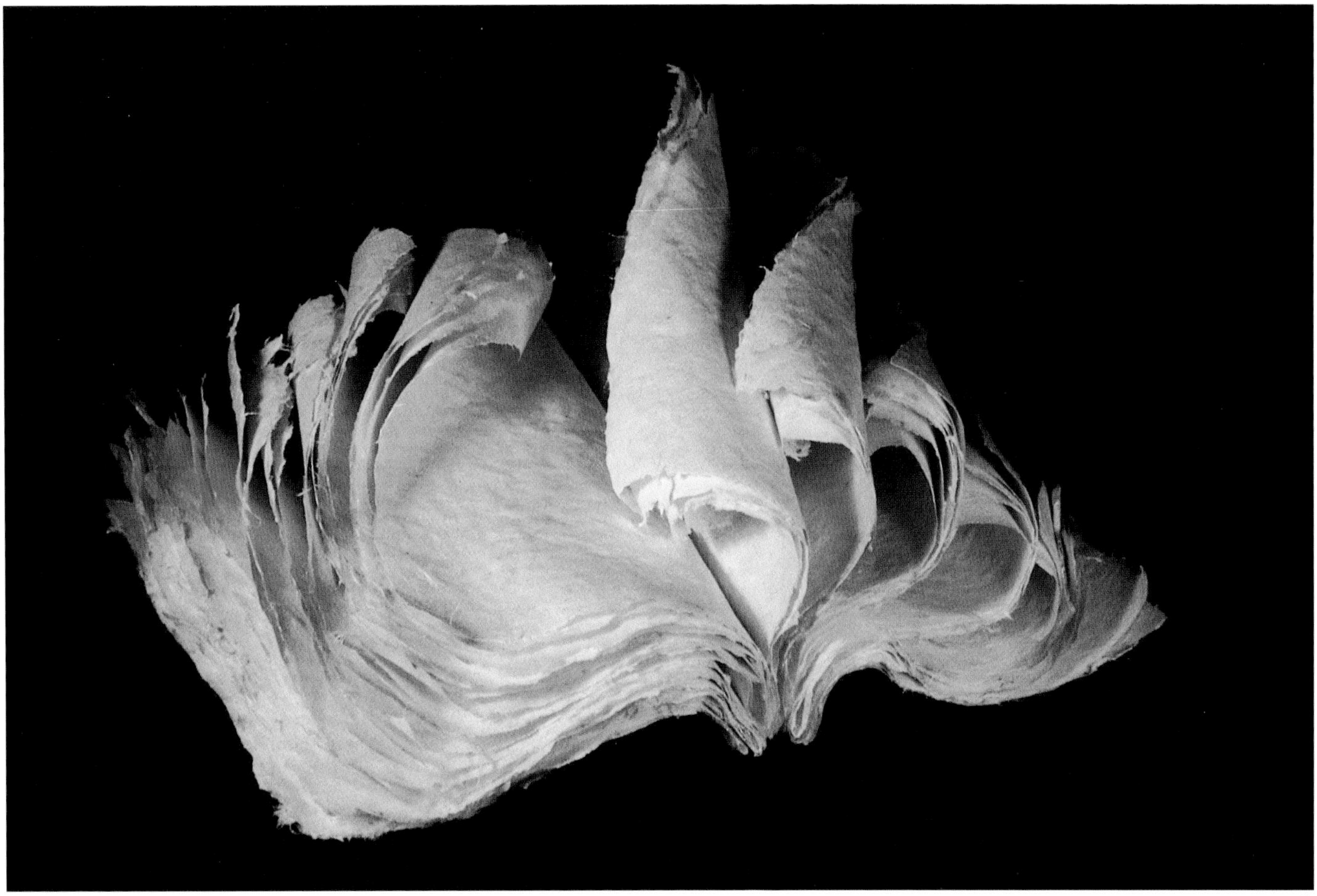

3

4

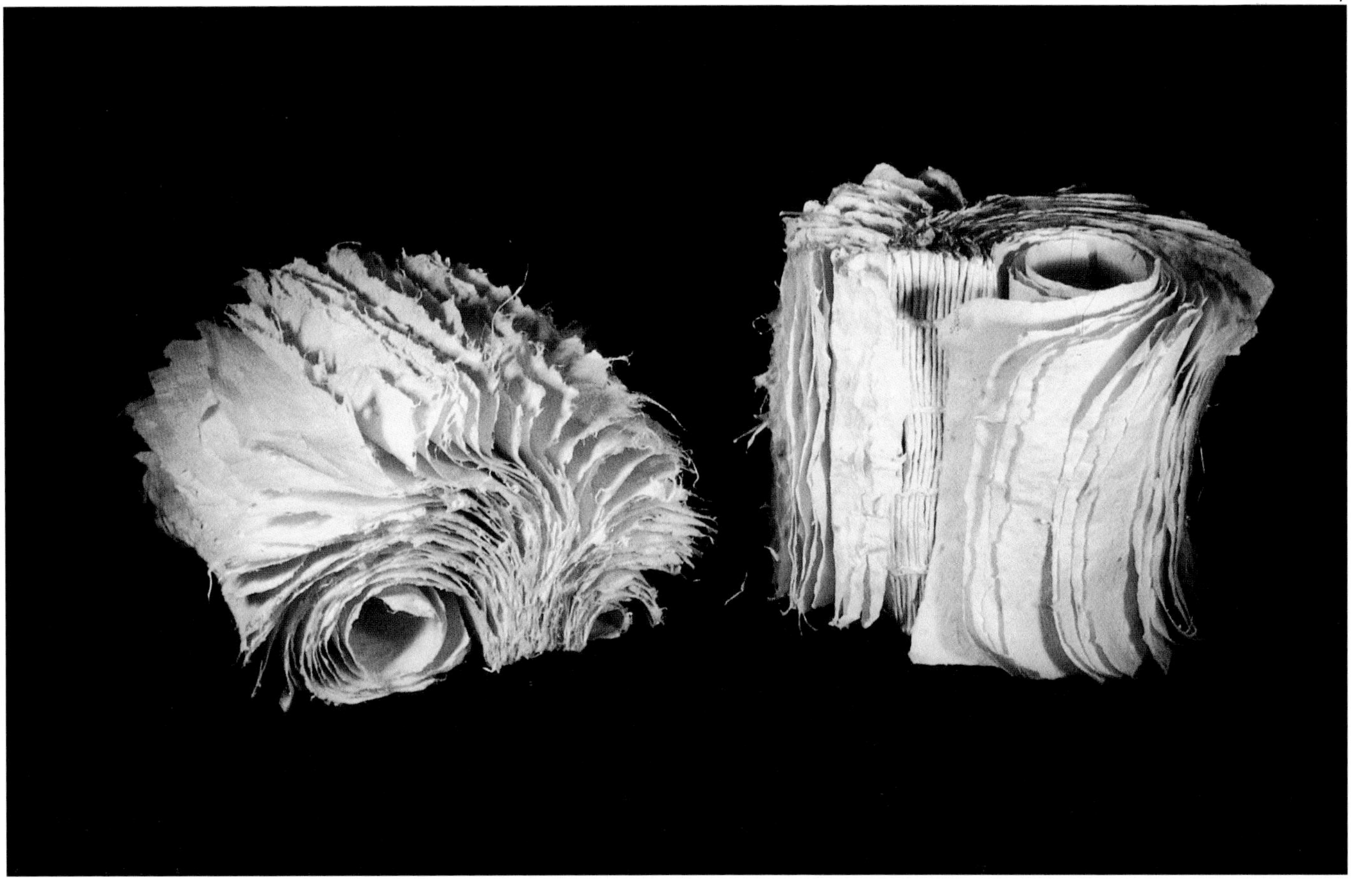

Yvonne Cabanis

2 Rue Ernest Renan, 30600 Vauvert, France

1

An artist of wearable* fine arts (in the Beaux-Arts training), I have been teaching fine arts, creativity, and subjectivity of color in the Robert Gourdon cultural center of Vauvert, as well as in state training institutions since 1974. I lead courses on color applied to a diverse range of materials: metal, fabric (worn), and in particular, paper in volume (hats), cloth as wall hangings, but also for the body, the head, etc.; by researching material, quantity, and colors to wear with courage and a good dose of silliness.

My participation in the organization of the fashion parade—an international competition called *Atout Fil* (Clothes Madness)—confirms for me the importance of the work being worn. After seeing and touching the work, wearing it reinforces the exchange between the creator and "the other," and in doing so, modifies our perception of it.

It doesn't matter if the work suffers by being worn—it lives. What's so important about the numerous exhibits over the course of the past century in galleries abroad? My living creations walk down the road in Japan, Australia, New York, England (Ascot), Paris (Longchamp, Bagatelle), Italy, Sweden, Germany . . .

In the summer of 2001, the museum of Arts de Reillanne (Alpes-de-Haute-Provence) and a hat museum in Chazelles-sur-Lyon welcomed my paper hats. A piece of clothing is still exhibited in Dordogne at Varaignes (the imaginary clothing exhibit), and a gardener's apron is in Paris. All that has been achieved, even if I, myself, remain soundly working in my workshop in Vauvert in the Camargue (while also appearing on the television from time to time!).

You can always come to see and try on my creations!

Yvonne Cabanis

2

* The notion of wearing is very important to me. A work that is worn, put on, assumes a life of its own and transforms itself. It may even enjoy international recognition if it is also exhibited in the street, museums, or galleries. The individual who is seduced by the work creates an additional source of exposure: one lives with the other.

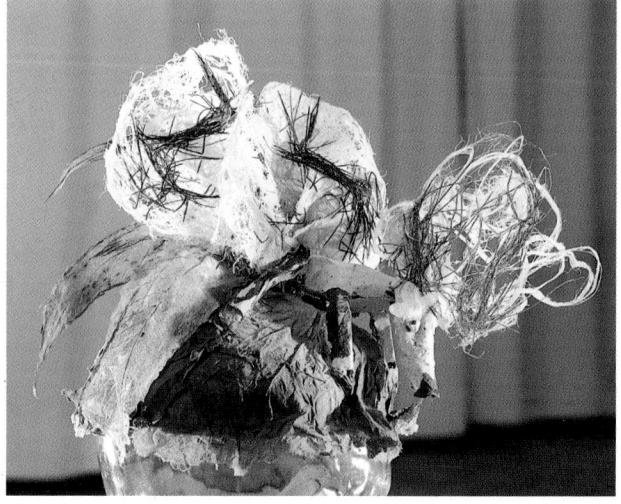

3

1. Untitled, 2002
2. Flying hat (plant paper, string made from craft paper, dried roses), 55 x 55 x 40 cm
3. The little climbing animal, 35 x 30 x 25 cm
4. Incantation (plant paper), 35 x 35 x 38 cm

Photographs: Yves Cavaillé (34070 Montpellier, France)

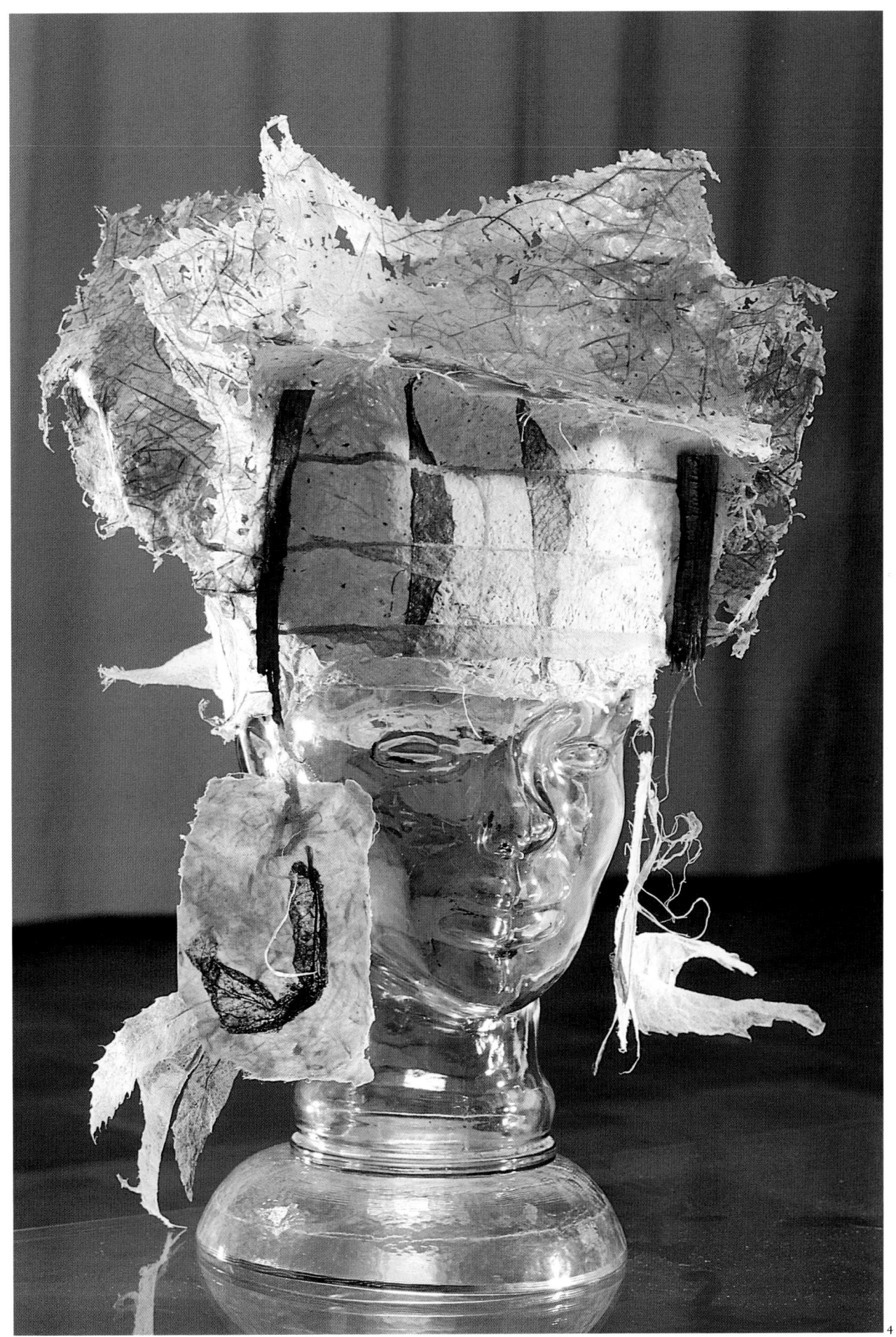

Marie-Thérèse Herbin

12 Rue Dubuc, 78120 Rambouillet, France

My technique for producing paper begins with the collection of plants: iris and daylily leaves, large rhubarbs, flax, or gladioli of Byzantium . . . always fibrous plants. Then comes the cauldron for a séance of stewing the plant, dyeing, rinsing, and macerating. Next is the traditional production of paper: the pulp expands as the mold and deckle suspends it on the surface of the water. The fibers become entangled in moving shapes. The screen is submerged in order to collect, one by one, these random compositions. The rest is only a matter of manipulation, assemblage, games, and wandering thoughts. A chronic calligrapher of plants: my suspended gardens congeal and dream of other tactile horizons.

Marie-Thérèse Herbin

Professor of design, Marie-Thérèse Herbin lives and works in Rambouillet, not far from Paris. She exhibits in the French capital but also in Barcelona, Quebec, and Japan. She participates in the Biennial of Flax and created forty original covers for Le Savoir de la terre, *by Pierre Oster Soussouev (published by Babel). She is also the illustrator of* l'Heure creuse *by Claude Louis-Combet (Babel).*

1. Trois savoirs (flax, rhubarb, recycled boxwood paper), 32 x 32 cm, 1998
2 and 3. Vegetable garden (combined techniques: vegetable fiber, recycled paper, glass bells, and wood), 400 x 150 x 100 cm, 1991/2001
4. Fragments adrift (flax and rhubarb), 70 x 62 cm, 1996

Photographs: Marie-Thérèse Herbin

160

Marie-Claire Meier

25 Vervas, 2520 La Neuveville, Switzerland

By transforming plant into paper, I find the language of fibers—which seems to be a universal language—the ideal instrument for communicating.

At a time of international communication on the Internet, paper is a privileged repository of non-verbal, intuitive writing because of its sensuality.

I create my own paper. I transform flax or cotton cloths, as papermakers in the Middle Ages did, using the Hollander beater, or I transform plants and their peels through a chemical process to guarantee a stable material, as papermakers in Japan still do today.

When working with straw, for example, I find the language of fibers the ideal instrument for raising questions that come to me.

When imbuing pieces of cotton with a "second life," it is the memory of the material that fascinates me, its fingerprint, its mark—all sorts of non-verbal communication that permit me to express myself.

The moment the Internet allowed for international communication, artists seemed to me to be the sentinels of tactile, non-verbal, intuitive communication. Paper is the privileged repository of this communication. All my work articulates itself around this theme: letters, signs, memories, dialogue, messages, prayers, meditations, taboos, or secrets . . .

Furthermore, producing my own paper pulp allows me to intervene at the most basic level and add diverse pigments, sand, marble powders, cinder, earth, fragments of text, and to emboss various structures on it.

From there, it is possible to combine all sorts of techniques (acrylic, oil, ink) or work within the space itself (sculptures). I spend much time researching and experimenting. Transforming material is a way of transforming oneself because in seeking the limits of the material, we discover our own.

Marie-Claire Meier

Born in 1952, Marie-Claire Meier lives and works in Switzerland. An instructor, she has maintained her own training, notably on the production of paper. She took an advanced course in textile art and received distinctions in the United States for her work with plant paper.

4

1. Personal letters (various papers, combined techniques), 70 x 70 cm
2. History (flax paper), 30 x 26 x 20 cm
3. (Installation) Pyramids (various papers: straw, asparagus, hay, etc.), from 100 to 160 cm
4. Promise (egg made from the silver dollar plant), 24 x 16 x 16 cm

Photographs: Marie-Claire Meier and Paul-André Duvoisin (Bôle, Switzerland)

Ruth Moro

Modino, 6654 Cavigliano, Switzerland

The world of plants is the framework for my search to discover, then express and realize, the multiple, hidden facets of this universe. Plants not only have a hidden soul, but also their own geometry and elementary order to uncover.

Paper is a voyage for me; a voyage through the kingdom of nature, but also an internal, contemplative voyage to uncover what is hidden and discover other plants and crops. I search for plants and investigate their world to reveal what is not apparent upon first glance—that is, this basic natural order, this element of origin that acts as their fundamental soul.

This element is the expression, the minimal alphabet with which I create and construct my work. By guiding and letting myself be guided by the qualities flowing from these elemental characteristics, the dialogue between nature and me is born.

Manipulating and reorganizing these elemental components—the alphabet suggested by the structure of plants—I create. The compositions are often complex, but the works that are born from them are not just paper; the qualities of the plants are present and my projects therefore assume their force, their autonomy, and their original language.

Ruth Moro

With a diploma in occupational therapy, and self-taught in the world of handmade paper and paper art, Ruth Moro attended courses and workshops in Switzerland, France, Holland, Germany, and Japan. She is a member of the International Association of Hand Papermakers and Paper Artists (IAPMA) as well as the Society of Visual Artists (Switzerland). Since 1997 her work has been exhibited in the European Union, Switzerland, and Japan.

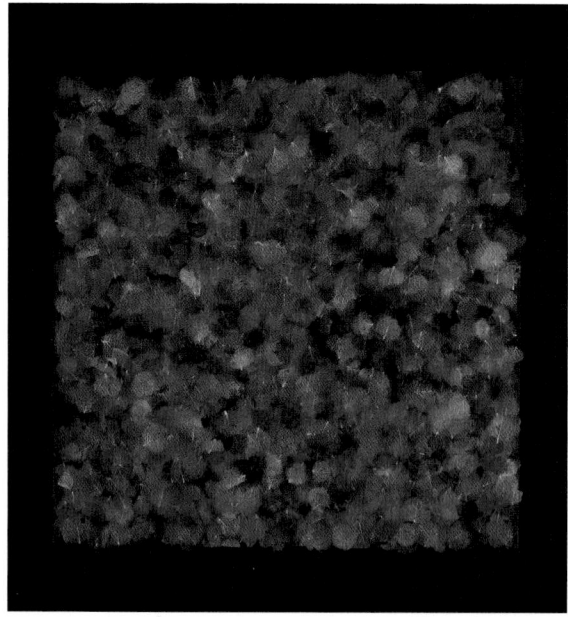

1

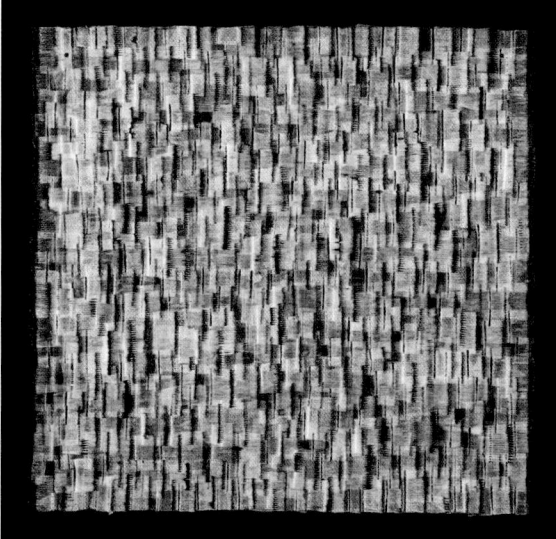

2

3

4

1. Photograms in blue (*Acer pseudoplatanus l.*), 30 x 30 x 5 cm, 1995
2. First snow (*Equisetum telmateia*), 30 x 30 cm, 1996
3. Embraces (*Acer pseudoplatanus l.*), 30 x 30 cm, 1997
4. Mythic journey (*Hydrangea quercifolia*), 30 x 30 cm, 1998

Photographs: Alberto Flammer (6653 Verscio, Switzerland)

Aurelia Muñoz

586 Gran Via, principal - 2°, 08011 Barcelona, Spain

1

I began the creation of artists' books and book objects in 1981 and to this day I continue to explore the possibilities of paper as material and as artistic expression.

With a knowledge of cultural and artistic textiles, I achieved a series of works in paper: artists' books, textile sculptures, miniatures, and large, three-dimensional mobiles and montages. In the initial period of work, until 1984, I worked with paper that was familiar to me but also with papers from other cultures, while adding color and primer, transforming and manipulating according to different methods.

Since 1984, I have worked with papers of various thickness starting from the pulp, particularly with flax: from delicate sheets to really thick paper of two or three layers.

You can dry the paper in a free manner to give it an irregular or organic form. In the same way, it is possible to achieve uniform forms with the help of pieces of wood that can be substituted for a more traditional mold. Then, putting the paper under various amounts of pressure makes the sheets regular and flat. Sometimes, by incorporating different elements in the pulp, like shells, sand, mica, or metallic dust, you can achieve results that enrich the material.

Once the paper is elaborated, you can achieve three-dimensional sculptures of different colors. Certain works—mobiles—float freely in space. Others are presented in Plexiglas cases.

In several of my works, particularly the mobiles, you can observe the references to textile by the introduction of threads, surface textures, and the sequence of these elements.

My most recent works are based on sketches or are created freely. Their parts can be put together like a puzzle, by playing with their forms, colors, and the tension between opacity and transparency through different types of paper.

2

Aurelia Muñoz

Aurelia Muñoz lives in Barcelona, where she was born in 1926. She has exhibited her work since 1963, first in Spain, then throughout the world. Since the 1970s, she has participated in the Biennial of Miniature Textiles in London, at the International Congress of Textile Research in Madrid, and at the International Exhibition of Paper Art in Budapest, among other places.

3

4

1. Reliquary (handmade flax paper), 32 x 36 x 6 cm, 1987
2. Lunar object (handmade flax paper), 51 x 51 x 51 cm, 1990
3. Oriental object (handmade flax paper), 36 x 67 x 14 cm, 1987
4. White algae (handmade flax paper), 38 x 45 x 8 cm, 1987

Photographs: F. Català-Roca (08024 Barcelona, Spain) and Rocco Ricci (08007 Barcelona, Spain)

Pascale Pasello

14 Allée de l'Affranchi, 91000 Evry, France

In 1997, in the footsteps of Alfred Manessier, Pascale Pasello moved to the bay of Somme in northern France. She collects driftwood with which she builds reliquaries and votive offerings.

In 2000, Marie-Jeanne Lorenté taught her the art of papermaking with plants. Since then, she has explored the artistic possibilities of this material in which pleasure resides in assiduous respect for the transformative process.

She calls her projects plant moltings. Her sculptures are made from the leaves of chestnut, oak, or elm, cooked and made into paper. The paper is then discolored, at times recolored, applied to manufactured forms, and pressed to allow it to be molded. After drying, the molting can be separated from its support.

Durably fragile, it is a representation of the invisible presence of what has left her soul.

As if ministering to the plant, there are precise gestures to follow: pick, cook, rinse, bleach, recolor, place, bend, press, incise, extract, stitch up and back together again.

In the end, it's "a new skin that reveals its bare, living self to us."

Éric Ferrari

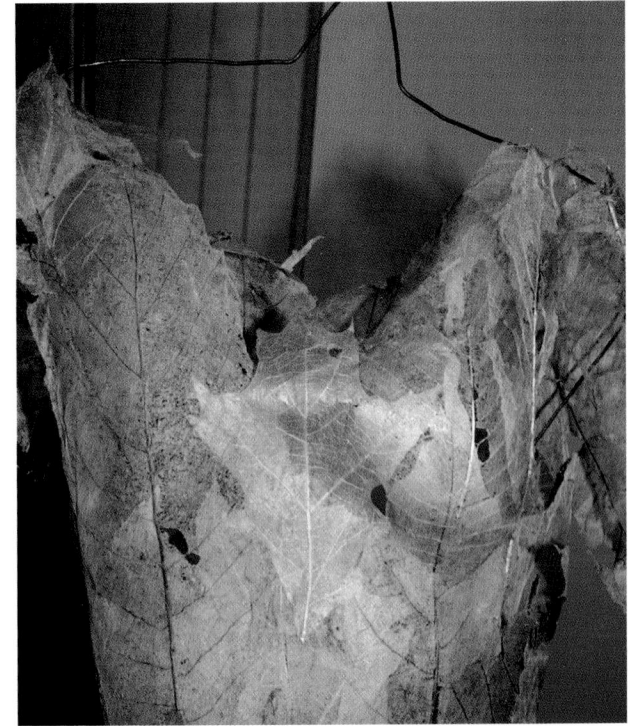

1

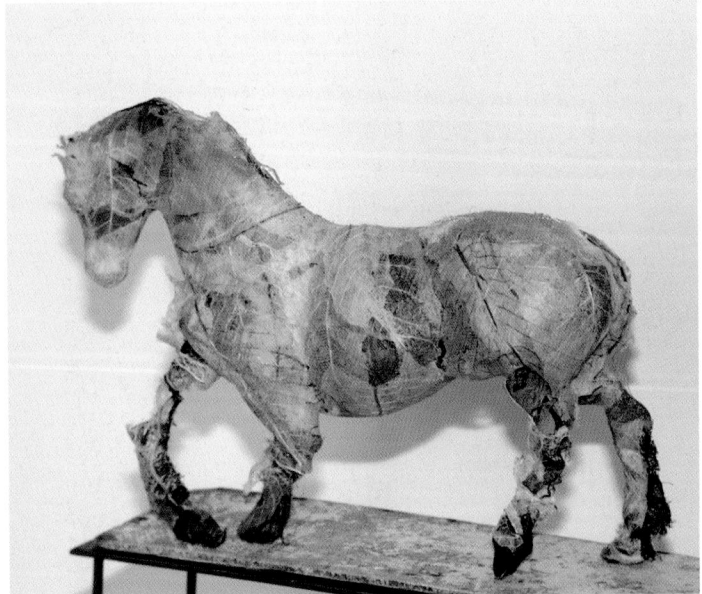

2

3

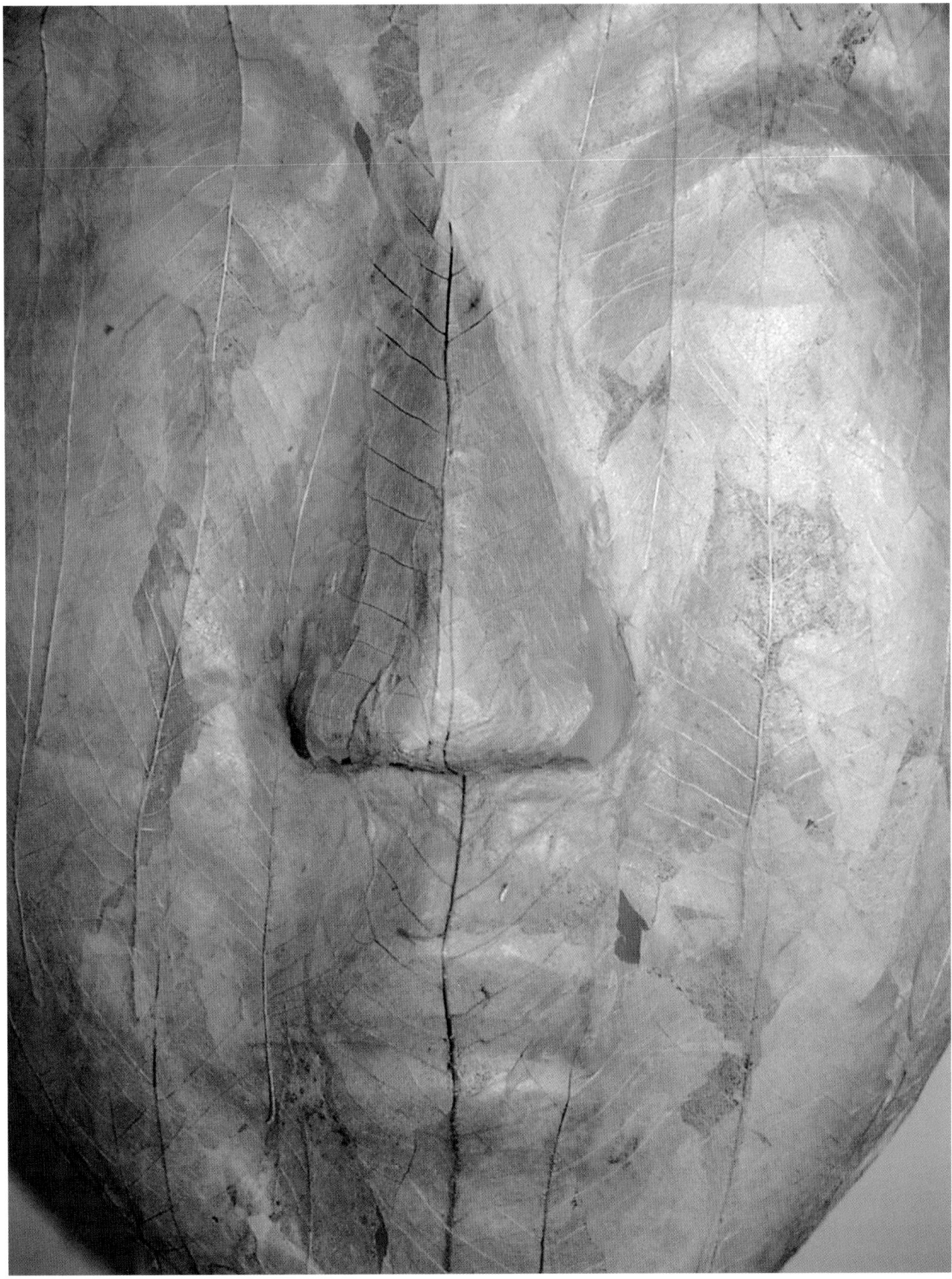

4

1. Detail of a sound body (chestnut tree leaves, human scale), 2001
2. Plant molting, the yellow horse (tarlatan and elm tree leaves), 25 x 30 cm, 2001
3. Plant molting, sound body (tarlatan and chestnut tree leaves), 50 x 35 cm, 2001
4. Mask (chestnut tree leaves), 2001

Photographs: Françoise Meyer-Jegou (02130 Beuvardes, France) and Frederick Devillard (91 Videlles, France)

Jean-Paul Ruiz

Le Roc, 19130 Saint-Aulaire, France

My work manifests itself around an ethic of life based on a complex thought process of the planetary environment, taking into account the natural and cultural conditions that can influence living organisms and human activities.

The artist's book enters into my expression of fine arts the same way as painting, video, and exhibits. Each book is conceived like a scenography in which the form, composition, graphic quality, impression, paper, material, and text (unedited, by order of the author) are all composed in order to illustrate the subject's concept. The texts are news, scientific reports, philosophical reflections, essays, and prose.

Jean-Paul Ruiz

Founding member of the Organization for the Use of Dew, a member of promotional associations for the artistic journal, and author, Jean-Paul Ruiz exhibited his work in the Centre Georges Pompidou in Paris in May 2001. He attends numerous European exhibits dedicated to books and especially to artistic journals.

1

1. Installation (paper sculpture, paper sediment, acrylic), 220 x 140 x 40 cm, 1993
2. Paper sheet (paper, string, rock), 32 x 40 x 30 cm)

Photographs: Jean-Paul Ruiz

Hiltrud Schäfer

5 Schürmannskamp, 49080 Osnabrück, Germany

Since 1988, the notion of "drawing forth from paper" has belonged to the artistic vocabulary of Hiltrud Schäfer. Her plant-based papers are proof of an impressive power.

Hiltrud makes paper from indigenous plants, namely sedge and kozo (the fiber of a Japanese mulberry). Because she performs all the steps herself—from seeking out the plants to exhibiting her work—she can intervene at any moment in order to achieve precisely what she wants for any given work.

The organic element of plants—the symbol of life and death—emerges through an irreversible fusion between the content and form of her installations.

In her works, Hiltrud Schäfer addresses the tension that reigns between birth and life, the ephemeral and death. The element of time becomes metaphorically attainable.

Some of her works specify this concept: *Ephemeral and Decomposition, Requiem, Everything at Its Own Time . . . , Funeral March*, etc.

André Lindhorst

Hiltrud Schäfer was born and lives today in Germany. She took specialized courses in plant paper in Belgium, Japan, Bolivia, and Taiwan. She is a member of the International Association of Hand Papermakers and Paper Artists (IAPMA), and exhibits in Germany and elsewhere.

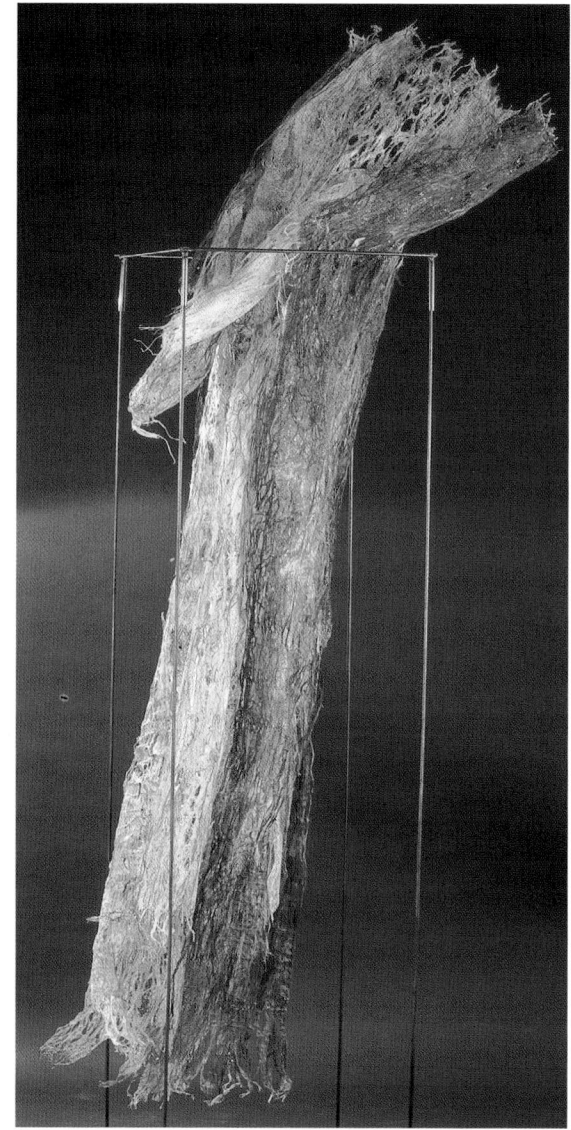

1

1. Haute (detail), 220 x 40 x 50 cm, 2000
2. Haute, 220 x 40 x 50 cm, 2000
3. Paar (detail), 210 x 120 x 50 cm, 1992

Photographs:
Henning Krause, Cologne, Germany
Maria Otte, Melle, Germany

2

Bibliography

Gaston Bonnier and George De Layens, *La Flore complète portative de la France, de la Suisse et de la Belgique,* Belin

Delachaux and Niestl, *La nature méditerranéenne en France,* Les Écologistes de l'Euzière

Les Cahiers de Médiologie, number 4
Pouvoirs du papier, review edited by Régis Debray,
Gallimard

Dominique and Michèle Fremy, *Quid 2001*, Robert Laffont

Françoise Paireau, *Japanese paper*, Adam Biro

Credits

Photographs by Vincent Decorde,
except where noted otherwise.

Black and white illustrations are taken from *Descriptive and illustrative flora of France, Corsica, and neighboring regions,* by Hippolyte Coste Abbey, Librarie des Sciences et Arts, Paris, 1937. We thank the Society of Sciences, Arts, and Letters of Aveyron for having entrusted us with this work.

The following black-and-white illustrations are by Sophie Beltran: eggplant, bamboo, canna, mushroom, cranberry bean, zucchini, gingko biloba, green beans, pampas grass, spiderwort, wasp nest, palm tree, papyrus, pumpkin, tomato, and yucca.

The watercolors are also by Sophie Beltran.

Thanks to:

all the artists mentioned in this book, who were immensely patient;
my children, who seem never to have doubted me;
Mr. Jarry, honorary professor at the Medical School of Montpellier and
curator of the Jardin des Plantes in Montpellier, for his availability and his technical help;
Françoise Martin for her practical help; Ghislaine Valette for her psychological help;
Claude Varisco for his knowledge of papermaking and his friendship; all my students who,
for ten years, shook me up in my pedagogical work; my editor for her tenacity; the
Heidelberg House in Montpellier; Philippe Martin of the Environmentalists
of the Euzière in Prades-le-Lez, Hérault,
and Ernest Pignon Ernest.